THE DANCE OF DEATH

Choreography and Dance Studies

A series of books edited by Robert P. Cohan, C.B.E.

This book is part of a series. The publisher will accept continuation orders which may be cancelled at any time and which provide for automatic billing and shipping of each title in the series upon publication. Please write for details.

THE DANCE OF DEATH.

Kurt Jooss and the Weimar Years

Suzanne K. Walther, S. K.

harwood academic publishers
Switzerland ● Australia ● Belgium ● France ● Germany ● Great Britain
India ● Japan ● Malaysia ● Netherlands ● Russia ● Singapore ● USA

Harwood Academic Publishers
Poststrasse 22
7000 Chur, Switzerland

British Library Cataloguing in Publication Data

Walther, Suzanne K.
  Dance of Death: Kurt Jooss and the Weimar
  Years. − (Choreography & Dance Studies,
  ISSN 0891-6381; Vol. 7)
  I. Title II. Series
  792.8092
  ISBN 3-7186-5532-2 (softback)
  ISBN 3-7186-5702-3 (hardback)

Dedicated to the forgotten victims of war

CONTENTS

Introduction to the Series

Choreography and Dance Studies is a book series of special interest to dancers, dance teachers and choreographers. Focusing on dance composition, its techniques and training, the series will also cover the relationship of choreography to other components of dance performance such as music, lighting and the training of dancers.

In addition, *Choreography and Dance Studies* will seek to publish new works and provide translations of works not previously published in English, as well as publish reprints of currently unavailable books of outstanding value to the dance community.

ROBERT P. COHAN

List of Plates

Acknowledgements

The writing of a book is not a solitary exercise. I am indebted to a great many people who provided me with guidance and encouragement and several institutions that furnished valuable material for use.

I am grateful to Anna Markard for sharing her understanding and knowledge of her father Kurt Jooss the artist and his ballets. She and her husband Hermann Markard gave me invaluable first-hand experience, insight and information. I thank Elsa Kahl Cohen who supplied me with significant research material from her personal archives. I am especially thankful to Dr. Patricia A. Row, Professor of Dance at New York University, for her advice in clarifying the bourne of the project. Gretchen Schumacher helped me to understand the complexities of Labanotation. Jean Cebron, Ernst Uthoff and Lola Botka generously shared their knowledge and memories. Selma Jeanne Cohen gave advice and encouragement, and Ernestine Stodelle helped in the unfolding of my aesthetic vision of dance.

I am grateful to my editors at Gordon and Breach: Robert Robertson for his infinite kindly patience, and Muriel Topaz for her generous encouragement. For the use of research material I thank the Dance Collection of The New York Public Library at Lincoln Center, The New York University Library, The Museum of Modern Art, The Dance Notation Bureau, and The Jooss Archives.

Finally I am most grateful to my husband Eric for his commitment and assistance from start to finish, my son Derek and my daughter Zenta for their interest and encouragement, and my friend Jonathan A. Weiss for assistance in manuscript preparation.

SUZANNE K. WALTHER

Introduction

The Weimar Republic was Germany's first democratic form of parliamentary government. The years between 1918 and 1933 were an extraordinary time of political turmoil, social change and cultural innovation. It was a time of artistic experimentation and intellectual ferment that initiated a European renaissance. It was also a time of unprecedented dance activity. Based on the practical philosophies and artistic ideas of Francois Delsarte, Emile Jaques Dalcroze, and Rudolf von Laban, a new movement emerged in the field. The advocates of the new dance promoted a more spontaneous physical expression of emotion than was permitted by the strict rules of the classical ballet.

During this time a young dancer-choreographer named Kurt Jooss attracted attention. By 1926 he had established a dance group called *Die Neue Tanzbühne* (The New Dance Stage). His sharp character sketches and keenly applied sense of humor revealed a deep psychological understanding of human nature. In 1932 the first international competition for choreographers was held in Paris. Jooss entered the competition with a work entitled *The Green Table*, and won first prize. This success catapulted him to instant world fame.

That *The Green Table* is a unique and enduring masterpiece is well established. Yet it is just one of the forty to fifty ballets choreographed by Jooss during his lifetime. Their subject matter varies from the ravages of war to the plight of the poor in modern industrial cities and the crushed spirit of the individual in an alienated society.

Jooss was concerned with how society could affect the life of the individual, and how society in turn was affected by the character and psychological make-up of its members. He was a master at depicting human character and devising movement that expressed the psychological motivation behind every action. At the same time, his characters became larger-than-life symbols of human actions. Critic Alan M. Storey, in an essay entitled "The Art of Kurt Jooss", observes that in the Jooss ballets "figures become units, soldiers become armies, brothels turn into nations where mental prostitution is rife and intelligence is dulled with craving for pleasure" (1940, p.596). Jooss's artistic creed, expressed in his own words, was "to give adequate form to genuine human expression" (quoted in Storey, 1940, p.596).

In the Jooss ballets, the dramatic content of the work shapes its choreographic form. Every gesture and step grows out of, and reveals, an inner experience of the protagonists. All movement is meaningful. For Jooss, dance is equated with theater. He said of his dances that "they are almost like plays, plays performed by movement instead of words." He explained that in his choreography "behind every movement there is an inner state, an inner emotion or idea, and the movement speaks of that inner experience." He considered this to be an application of Rudolf von Laban's study of the relationship between movement and emotion. In an interview, Jooss explained:

> In an uninhibited body with free flow, there is a continuous relationship between the emotion and movement, so we say there is no movement without psychological background. There should be no psychological tension without corresponding movement. (Gruen, 1976)

Interpretations of the cultural history of the Weimar Republic have placed little emphasis on the contributions of German modern dance, and of Kurt Jooss in particular, to the Weimar cultural period. This neglect needs correcting. Theatrical dance is a major art form, and Jooss belonged to that handful of outstanding artistic innovators who defined the Weimar culture and its contributions to history. Jooss himself made major contributions to dance technique, dance pedagogy and dance aesthetics.

The dance technique that Jooss developed was the first to fuse elements of modern dance with the basic principles of classical ballet. As founding director of the Folkwang School in Essen, Germany, he formulated a curriculum that included classical ballet, modern dance, folk dance, dance notation and teacher training. His writings and interviews, his method of training dancers and his own choreography all point to a coherent aesthetic theory of dance. He was an advocate of the professional theater and a proponent of *Gesamtkunstwerk* or "total art". He deliberately combined staging, costume, design, music and movement to create a complete work of art. Jooss was an active participant in the Weimar culture, and through his contributions and talent he decisively influenced the course of German dance.

There exists some controversy in the dance literature concerning whether Jooss was an Expressionist. Critics have often referred to him as "the Expressionist choreographer", but this label is valid only when the term is applied loosely in referring to a set of traits that are characteristic of most modern German art. When used with more precise reference to a distinctive movement in German art, the term Expressionist does not correctly apply to Jooss. This conclusion is supported by the analysis of his works presented here, and confirmed by the study of his aesthetic philosophy.

Although some Expressionist themes can be found in Jooss's works and especially in the ballet *The Green Table*, the objective manner of presentation and the orientation toward social problems points clearly to the post-Expressionist movement known as *Die Neue Sachlichkeit*, The New Objectivity. Humor, irony, caricature and realistic drama were Jooss's expressive tools. His work represents a rediscovery of aesthetic form; economy and restraint are achieved by an exclusive concentration on what is essential.

Jooss's choreographic technique was based on the theory that dance movement communicates directly through metakinesis, or the reciprocity between the psychological and the physical. He regarded the body as an expressive whole that participated in every gesture. Each movement in his ballets carried a dramatic value, a meaning controlled by an inner impulse. The dramatic expression was all in the choreography. He looked for the significant movement that would convey the essence of a character, his emotions and actions, and his relationship to others within society. He believed in a clear, theatrically legible dance form, a unified theme, balanced composition and the harmonious blend of elements.

Jooss was a social critic with humanistic concerns. He depicted the individual in the context of society; his characters were part of a milieu. He did not moralize or judge, but focussed attention on social realities. The influence of his inventions, theories and teaching is evident in the German *Tanztheater* and in other progressive tendencies in the dance world of today.

CHAPTER I: THE WEIMAR BACKGROUND

Kurt Jooss composed his greatest choreographies in the last years of the Weimar Republic. The Weimar period was deeply scarred by the unprecedented sufferings of the First World War and its bitter aftermath: a political and social dividedness that proved unresolvable and led directly to the Second World War. The far reaching dimensions of this political turmoil and instability greatly affected the cultural inventiveness and artistic originality of the period. It is necessary to comprehend the extent to which the Weimar culture was shaped by its politics in order to put Jooss's work in proper perspective. The Jooss aesthetic called upon the artist to present a clear and unblinking view of social reality. Nowhere has this been more dramatically realized than in the Jooss masterpiece, *The Green Table*, with its portrayal of wartime suffering and between-wars cynicism. Inevitably, the path to an understanding of Jooss's art begins with the Weimar Republic.

Weimar: The Fragile Republic

Germany lost World War I late in the summer of 1918. In the months that followed, political events moved fast. On September 30, General Erich von Ludendorff and Field Marshal Paul von Hindenburg informed Kaiser Wilhelm II of the defeat (Laqueur, 1980, p.1). The government formally asked for an armistice on October 3. The Emperor temporized until November 9. Then, faced with a spreading navy mutiny at the North Sea port of Kiel and resulting unrest in Berlin, he reluctantly abdicated his throne and fled to Holland. In the prevailing political vacuum, the Social Democrat Philipp Scheidemann immediately proclaimed a Republic. After more than four years of a bloody and devastating war in which nearly two million Germans were killed and four million wounded (Friedrich, 1972, p.15), the armistice was signed at Compiegne on November 11.[1]

Count Harry Graf Kessler recorded in his meticulously kept diary:[2]

> So closes this first day of the revolution which has witnessed in
> a few hours the downfall of the Hohenzollerns, the dissolution
> of the German Army, and of the old order of society in Germany.

1

One of the most memorable and dreadful days in German history. (Kessler, 1971, p.9)

Scheidemann's bold political step had been hastened by the threat posed by the Marxist Karl Liebknecht.[3] It was feared that he would proclaim a Soviet Republic, reducing Germany in effect to a province of Communist Russia (Gay, 1968, p.11).

The city of Weimar became the choice for the first constitutional assembly held on February 9, 1919. The next day the Provisional Constitution was approved (Kessler, 1971, p.67) and two days later Friedrich Ebert was elected President. By August 11, the new Constitution became law (Gay, 1974, p.158). Thus was born Germany's first parliamentary regime, the Weimer Republic, a democratic form of republican government.

The main reason for the choice of Weimar as the new political capital and the site for the constituent assembly was that Berlin was considered unsafe after the war. Another reason was that, as the city of Goethe, Weimar represented for Germans "humanist philosophy" and "pacific cosmopolitanism" (Gay, 1974, p.1). In spite of the admirable sentiments accompanying its creation, historian Peter Gay aptly states that "The Republic was born in defeat, lived in turmoil, and died in disaster" (Gay, 1974, p.1).

In 1914, Europeans had welcomed the war with patriotic fervor. The armies marched off in the spirit of adventure. Governments and people were equally filled with nationalistic enthusiasm and military zeal. At that time no one foresaw the large-scale disaster that the war would become for all participants. After the particularly devastating maritime expedition at the Dardanelles, Winston Churchill wrote with prophetic foresight:

> Thereafter events passed very largely outside the scope of conscious choice. Governments and individuals conformed to the rhythm, of the tragedy, and swayed and staggered forward in helpless violence, slaughtering and squandering on ever-increasing scales, till injuries were wrought to the structure of human society which a century will not efface, and which may conceivably prove fatal to the present civilization. (Garraty & Gay, 1972, p.985)

No one had foreseen how drastically the recent technological advances in weaponry and war machinery would multiply and extend the horror and suffering of combat. By the end of the first year the vast armies of the western front were dug in and stalemated. Their trenches faced each other across a narrow strip of no man's land, and they remained so for four years, to the very end of the war.

In *All Quiet on the Western Front*, the most awesome literary document of the time, Erich Maria Remarque describes the conditions on the front:

> Shells, gas clouds, and flotillas of tanks — shattering, corroding, death. Dysentery, influenza, typhus — scalding, choking, death. Trenches, hospitals, the common grave — there are no other possibilities. The summer of 1918 is the most bloody and the most terrible. The days stand like angels in blue and gold,

incomprehensible, above the ring of annihilation. Every man here knows that we are losing the war. (Remarque, 1975, p.246)

The German army used poison gas on land and zeppelins for air raids, while England invented armored vehicles that became known as tanks. At first the Germans considered the tank a "mechanical toy" until they realized its capabilities. Remarque, who writes from his own experience as a soldier in the German army, says: "From a mockery the tanks have become a terrible weapon. Armored, they come rolling on in long lines, more than anything else embodying for us the horror of war" (1975, p.244). From this devastating horror which was filled with death, hopelessness and the senselessness of it all, the survivors emerged with physical and emotional wounds that were often permanent.

The trauma of the war and especially of combat service was reflected by the intense reactions of the artists who observed, recorded, and bore witness to the times. The painter George Grosz, who was discharged from the army and declared permanently unfit for service for psychological reasons, wrote in his autobiography:

I went back to live in Berlin. The city looked like a gray corpse made of stone. There were cracks in all the walls. Plaster and paint were crumbling. The dead, dirty, hollow windows seemed still to be mourning for whom they had looked in vain. (Grosz, 1983, p.113)

In sardonic caricature, he drew the unspeakable misery of the city's war-ravaged inhabitants, the dirty, frightened, lonely men mutilated in combat, the prostitutes, the poor, the starving children. He drew the war cripples without noses, with artificial arms, emaciated and reduced to begging. He drew the brutality of the military and the civilians alike, executions, suicide and murder.

In similar bitterly mocking style, Bertold Brecht in his famous poem "Legend of the Dead Soldier" told the bizarre tale of a soldier's corpse. It is dug up by army medics, who pour schnapps into it, deodorize it with incense and declare it fit to fight. They promptly send it back to the front to once again die a "hero's death" for the fatherland (Bentley, 1981, p.25).

Although the soldiers carried the main burden, the war affected everyone. The painter Käthe Kollwitz, who lost her eighteen-year-old son in the first few months of battle, produced many deeply moving drawings, among them a lithograph of a woman engulfed in sorrow entitled *Das Warten (The Waiting)* (Willett, 1984, p.23). Dancer-choreographer Mary Wigman created *Totenmal* (1930), a choric dance about death. In her book *The Language of Dance* she explains how the work was inspired by women's mourning for their loved ones killed in the war:

Fear, horror, terror, pain, and despair of death — the experience of women was burdened with all these images of war, while the male chorus stood in the realm of the forgotten, never again to be reached by anything. There was no longer any love nor the understanding of human demands. (Wigman, 1966, pp.93–94)

The event which dealt a crushing political blow to this ravaged country was the signing of the peace treaty at Versailles. Not until then did the German people realize the extent of their defeat and humiliation. The terms of the treaty were so unfavorable to Germany that Scheidemann resigned the Chancellorship rather than sign it.

Germany lost the important industrial territory of Alsace-Lorraine to France, and the coal mining region of Silesia to Poland. Denmark and Belgium took some border territories, and the African colonies were assigned for administration to the League of Nations. Germany was forbidden to have an army beyond 100,000 men, and was allowed no tanks or warplanes. An astronomical sum was fixed by a Reparations Committee for Germany to pay to the Allies for war damages.

In article 231 of the treaty, Germany was made to acknowledge formally that the war was a sole consequence of her aggression, and that she was responsible for all the damage caused (Gay, 1974, pp.15–16). This "war guilt clause," as it came to be known, was a colossal moral burden to bear. Germany prided herself for the tradition of *Bildung* – "the formation of a cultured and civilized humanity" (Willett, 1984, p.14). This self-image contrasted sharply with the way the rest of the world saw the country. The Allies considered Germany a sinner against humanity in general and against Western Culture in particular.

The treaty was signed under the threat of renewed hostilities and invasion by the Allies. The war was over, but peace did not arrive. On January 10, 1920, Count Kessler made the following entry in his diary:

> Today the Peace Treaty was ratified at Paris; the War is over.
> A terrible era begins for Europe, like the gathering of clouds before
> a storm, and it will end in an explosion probably still more terrible
> than that of the World War. In Germany there are all the signs
> of a continuing growth of nationalism. (Kessler, 1971, p.117)

The terrible suffering endured by the German people during the war years came to have an ambiguous meaning after the difficult years that followed. The brilliant journalist Kurt Tucholsky warned in his articles that the white spots left on the wall of the German Military Academy by the frequently posted casualty lists had one unmistakable meaning: "No more wars!" But not even Tucholsky believed that his warning would be heeded. As Churchill predicted, the seeds of future trouble had been sown in the magnitude of the atrocities of the war.

Much later, when Kurt Jooss was asked about the political content of his anti-war ballet *The Green Table,*[4] his answer reflected the loss of faith in a secure world and the premonition of yet worse to come that grew up during the Weimar period. He referred to Tucholsky in describing his feelings:

> At the time (1932) I was reading a lot in a German periodical called
> "Die Weltbühne". It was run by Carl von Ossietzky, and one of
> the main writers was Kurt Tucholsky. He was a very great man,
> a political journalist, who incessantly said in his writing: "Don't
> believe it, these peace talks. It's all rubbish, it's all fake, they are
> secretly preparing a new war." (Markard & Markard, 1985, p.49)

German nationalism was built on militarism, but it also included the cultural traditions of philosophy, music, literature and poetry, a pride in the classical heritage and a belief in the "civilizing mission of the German people." The moral burden of war guilt caused undue stress in the national psyche. Opposition to it gave rise to a whole ideology with a false premise, an explanation for the loss of the war. According to this unrealistic theorizing, the war was lost because hidden forces at the highest levels of the nation had betrayed Germany to the enemy. This became known as the "stab in the back" theory. The members of the first provisional government of the Republic, formed on November 10, were later referred to as the "November criminals." This myth played a central role in conservative propaganda and was eventually exploited by Hitler and the Nazis (Laqueur, 1980, p.5).

Political conservatism in Germany included the belief in a centralized government with a strong leader. Parliamentary democracy was considered to be a foreign import, unsuited to the country's need for unity. While the majority supported the new constitution, the extremists viewed the Weimar Republic with suspicion from the beginning (Laqueur, 1980, p.6). Both the right-wing conservatives and the left-wing liberals tried their utmost to overthrow the fragile new political system.

First a group of left-wing Marxists led by Karl Liebknecht and Rosa Luxemburg, calling themselves the Spartacists, staged an unsuccessful revolution in Berlin. On January 15, 1919, both leaders were captured and brutally murdered (Friedrich, 1972, pp.45–46). Gustav Noske, the new head of the War Ministry, used the newly formed *Freikorps* to smash the Communist revolution. The *Freikorps* was a paramilitary organization made up of right-wing ex-military men, drifters, and various youthful adventurers, all without scruples and eager to fight and kill. Internal violence continued. Kurt Eisner, the Bavarian Prime Minister, was assassinated. Scheidemann narrowly escaped being blinded by an assailant who threw acid in his face.

Then a conservative Prussian bureaucrat, Dr. Wolfgang Kapp, entered into a conspiracy with Generals Walther von Luttwitz and Ludendorff. They attempted to overthrow the regime with the help of a naval brigade and to install Dr. Kapp as chancellor. The Kapp Putsch lasted four days, during which a general strike paralyzed all governmental functions to the point that Kapp had to resign (Friedrich, 1972, p.64). The next chancellor, Joseph Worth, appointed Walther Rathenau to the post of foreign minister. The Jewish financier took office on January 31, 1922. On June 24 he was assassinated by three young right-wing militants, hit by five bullets as he rode to work in his open car (Friedrich, 1972, p.113). Rathenau's murderers reached appropriately ignominious ends. In many less notorious cases, however, conservative judges failed to mete out punishment to right-wing thugs charged with the killing of communists and socialists.[5]

Meanwhile inflation mounted. When Germany was unable to make timely payment of reparations to France, French and Belgian troops occupied the industries and mines of the Ruhr in January 1923. The German workers mounted a campaign of passive resistance to the occupation, and production nearly stopped. Inflation went out of control, food became scarce, people lost their savings, and the black market profiteers became rich. Draconian measures of economy were taken to stabilize the mark, but the economic hardship and political uncertainty continued (Gay, 1974, p.162).

On November 9, 1923, a small group of unknown politicians, led once again by the conspiratorial army hero General Ludendorff, staged an unsuccessful putsch at Munich. The leaders of this "beer-hall putsch" (as it came to be known) were captured, tried, and convicted of high treason. The main defendant was Adolf Hitler, a leading member of the extreme right-wing anti-Semitic party called the National Socialist German Workers' Party. An obscure political figure with a penchant for oratory, his impassioned speeches turned the trial into an anti-Republican propaganda display (Shirer, 1960, pp.71–79).

Hitler was sentenced to five years in prison, though he served less than one. He used the time of his confinement in Landsberg prison to set down his political ideas and half-baked theories on various topics in a book eventually given the title *Mein Kampf*.[6] As historian William L. Shirer notes:

> The blueprint of the Third Reich and, what is more, of the barbaric New Order which Hitler inflicted on conquered Europe in the triumphant years between 1939 and 1945, is set down in all its appalling crudity at great length and in detail between the covers of this revealing book. (Shirer, 1960, p.81)

However, it was ten years before Hitler was to come to power. In 1923 he was considered to be one dissatisfied crank among the many.

The years between 1923 and 1929 offered a measure of stability and relative prosperity. They are often referred to as the "golden twenties." When President Ebert died in 1925 he was succeeded by Field Marshal von Hindenburg, elected by a large majority at the polls (Gay, 1974, p.156). Most importantly, Gustav Stresemann became Foreign Minister. He engineered rapprochement in foreign relations and brought about a coalition of the numerous splinter parties in domestic politics (Friedrich, 1972, p.136).

According to a plan devised by the American banker Charles G. Dawes, France agreed to evacuate the Ruhr and Germany received some badly-needed foreign loans. Several important treaties were concluded in the years that followed. In 1925 the treaty at Locarno settled the Western frontiers of Germany. In 1926 a friendship treaty with Communist Russia was signed, and during the same year Germany entered the League of Nations. In 1928 the Kellogg-Briand Pact was concluded in which "nations renounced war as an instrument of national policy" (Garraty & Gay, 1972, p.1007).[7] Most of the postwar tensions were thus dissolved, and a period of economic boom ensued. Nevertheless, the sinister undercurrents of militarism and right-wing fanaticism remained in effect.

Unfortunately a caustic industrialist named Alfred Hugenberg, who made his fortune during the inflation, nearly monopolized the propaganda industry. An arch conservative, violently opposed to any reconciliation with the Allies, he joined forces with Hitler. Through his propaganda machine, the Austrian amateur painter became a prominent figure in national politics for the first time. But what finally gave Hitler the opportunity to gain the support of both the masses and the politicians in power was the oncoming economic depression.

The Great Depression in the United States which began with the Wall Street crash of 1929 had a world-wide effect. No country was more vulnerable to economic crisis than Germany, a country deeply in debt and dependent on foreign capital. Economic collapse was inevitable with the withdrawal of credit, the calling in of loans, and the end of foreign investment. Unemployment soared, hunger grew, and with it grew political discontent (Friedrich, 1972, p.300). The "golden twenties" were over.

Stresemann was gravely ill and died on October 24, 1929. His successor Hermann Müller also died within a year. Dr. Heinrich Brüning, head of the Catholic Center Party, succeeded him in office. He soon acquired the nickname "The Chancellor of Hunger" because of his severe austerity program. For most of his tenure he ruled by presidential decree, since the Parliament failed to agree on his financial plans (Friedrich, 1972, pp. 310–311).[8]

Meanwhile Hindenburg grew too old to govern effectively. He was eighty-six and had spells of memory lapse. The annual September rallies of the Nazi Party in Nüremberg grew in size and fervor. The SA (*Stürmabteilung* or Storm Troopers) under Captain Ernst Röhem became the largest military force in Germany. Brüning resigned, and his successor, the blundering Franz von Papen, lifted the existing ban on the Storm Troopers. He dissolved the Reichstag and called for new elections, in which the Nazis gained a plurality. The aging Hindenburg disliked Hitler, and called him "the little Austrian corporal," but the pressure mounted and he eventually yielded to the influence of his corrupt son Oskar von Hindenburg and von Papen.[9] On January 30, 1933, acting against his better judgment, Hindenburg swore in Hitler as Chancellor of the German Reich (Shirer, 1960, p.4).

Years earlier, during a court appearance, Hitler had declared in an inflammatory speech:[10]

> "I can assure you that when the National Socialist movement is victorious in this struggle, then there will be a National Socialist Court of Justice too. Then the November 1918 revolution will be avenged and heads will roll!" (Shirer, 1960, p.141)

Arthur Koestler, who lived in Berlin at the time, recounts in his autobiography an anecdote that reveals most accurately the spirit of this time. A Chinese executioner had the ambition of beheading a person with a stroke so swift that the victim's head would remain in place. When he finally achieved it and his victim asked, "Oh cruel Wang Lun, why do you prolong my agony of waiting?" he answered: "Kindly nod, please." Koestler continues:

> We walked along the hushed corridors of our citadel of German democracy [the publishing house of Ullstein], greeting each other with a grinning "Kindly nod please." And we fingered the back of our necks to make sure that the head was still solidly attached to it. The Weimar Republic was doomed. (Koestler, 1969, pp. 300–301)

On March 21, 1933, Hitler ceremoniously opened the first Reichstag of the Third Reich (Shirer, 1960, p. 197), and a new installment of the dark ages descended upon Europe. This is mainly true in terms of political history, but it applies to some degree to the history of the arts as well. For much more than a series of political events had been involved in giving definition to the Weimar Republic. The era of social change and cultural turmoil had been accompanied by unrivalled artistic creativity and experimentation. In the Weimar culture, modernistic trends in the arts gained wider acceptance than ever before. The avant-garde flourished, and the more prominent of the new artistic movements affected the future in ways that are still being worked out in dance and theater today.

The Beginning of Modernism

Kurt Jooss was initially attracted to the field of dance by a charismatic innovator, Rudolf von Laban. As he matured, Jooss absorbed the remarkably diverse artistic tendencies of the day and reshaped Laban's nearly mystical conceptions of movement into a disciplined and realistic aesthetic of dance theater. A proper understanding of his achievement requires that we first trace the beginnings of modernism in Germany and its multifarious bloomings in the arts of the Weimar period.

Political revolution seldom coincides exactly with cultural rebellion; the boundaries of modernism in the arts differ from the historical boundaries of the Weimar period (Laqueur, 1980, p.110). The roots of the modern artistic trends in Germany go back to the conservative Wilhelmian era before the war. Nonetheless, the intellectual ferment and artistic experimentation that Germany experienced during the few years of the Weimar Republic are probably unequalled in history.

The initiative to break with artistic tradition began at the turn of the century, spurred on by boredom and distaste for the prevailing academic schools. George Grosz wrote in his autobiography about his experience as a student at the Dresden Royal Academy of Art:

> Our main work was copying plaster casts in their original size; we had to deliver one every two weeks. Former lithographers were the best workers. They would make exact copies that included every minute accidental scratch or scrape, to the delight of our instructors who themselves were masters of such detail. As we did nothing but copy those boring plaster busts, the work was getting pretty stale. Anybody with inherent talent would seek satisfaction elsewhere. (Grosz, 1983, p.52)

Dissatisfied artists formed avant-garde groups under such names as *Die Brücke* and *Der Blaue Reiter (The Bridge* and *The Blue Rider)*. Poets and writers formed literary circles and founded new journals named *Der Sturm* and *Die Aktion (The Storm* and *The Action)*. The editor of *Der Sturm,* Herwarth Walden, also established a new art gallery. In an essay entitled "What is 'Der Sturm'?" Lothar Schreyer, a young artist and playwright who published in the journal, explained:

What was Der Sturm? A journal, an exhibition, a publishing house, an art school, a stage – but that doesn't cover it. It was not a society of artists, not an organization. It was a kind of turning point in European art. (Raabe, 1974, p.193)

By 1910, what had started out as a vague discontent with the existing conditions crystallized into a movement of opposition (Allen, 1983, p.18). In the following year the new movement received the name Expressionism in an article in Walden's periodical (Friedrich, 1970, p.153).

Even today, a precise definition of Expressionism eludes us (Allen, 1983, p.2). Willett offers both narrow and broad meanings for the term Expressionism:

1) A family characteristic of modern Germanic art, literature, music and theater, from the turn of the century to the present day.
2) A particular modern German movement which lasted roughly from 1910 until 1922.
3) A quality of expressive emphasis and distortion which may be found in works of art of any people or period. (Willett, 1970, p.8)

In spite of its short existence as a particular movement, Expressionism was perhaps the most far-reaching artistic influence in Weimar culture.

Other modernistic trends in the arts included Cubism, Futurism and the short-lived Dada movement, Constructivism and agit-prop Socialist Realism, the post-Expressionist movement called *Die Neue Sachlichkeit* (The New Objectivity), and a new architectural pragmatism characterized by the Bauhaus. The Bauhaus itself represented a unique experiment, quite readily accommodating artists from all of the "ism's" as teachers. By a collective effort they aimed at realizing the goal of reuniting architecture with the arts and crafts (Willett, 1984, pp.10; 13).

The contributions of independent artists and thinkers, creative minds not aligned with any movement, were also of vital importance to the intellectual life of the period. The German philosopher Martin Heidegger originated existential phenomenology, a movement that transformed European philosophy. He idealized the German language as the most suitable for expressing philosophical thought (Grene, 1967, p.459).[11] Albert Einstein, who had published his paper on the general theory of relativity in 1915, became a professor at the University of Berlin and was accepted as a member of the Prussian Academy of Sciences (Friedrich, 1972, p.56). Thomas Mann won the Nobel Prize for literature in 1929. His masterpiece *The Magic Mountain,* published in 1924, is an argument for rationalism in the face of decadence endangering Western culture (Laqueur, 1980, p.123). The collapse of Western civilization was explored in Oswald Spengler's apocalyptic philosophical history *The Decline of the West,* published in 1911.

On an entirely new front of human understanding, the study of psychoanalysis was already being pursued at the newly established Psychoanalytical Society in Berlin by 1910. The Society was founded by a close associate of Sigmund Freud. In 1920 it became the Psychoanalytic Institute of Berlin, where the teachers included such world-renowned analysts as Theodor Reich and Helene Deutsch (Laqueur, 1980, pp.213–214). Freud

himself gave a lecture at the Berlin Congress in 1922 in which he outlined
the structural basis for psychoanalysis: the superego, the ego, and the id
(Gay, 1974, p.36). Both phenomenology and psychology have greatly
influenced contemporary art.

In addition, the greatly expanded influence of popular culture, centered
mainly in Berlin, gave a special dazzle to the era. This mass culture included
modern jazz, the cinema, the cafes and cabarets – and, outside of the city,
the cults of sunbathing and physical culture. Not all modernism originated
in Germany or during the Weimar Republic, but it was during this period
that the avant-garde first entered into the mainstream of artistic and
intellectual life, bequeathing a rich heritage with lasting consequences for
contemporary culture.

In the visual arts the concepts of shape, form and color were liberated.
The Expressionist artists of *Die Brucke* were inspired by the primitive art
of Africa and the South Sea islands, by Etruscan sculpture and vases, and
by medieval wood carvings. The group was established in 1905 in Dresden
by the young artists Ernst Kirchner, Eric Heckel and Karl Schmidt-Rottluff
(Miesel, 1970, p.13).[12] They strove to link various art forms and to bridge
the gap between the avant-garde and the public. While their paintings
remained representational, they were influenced in the use of wild colors
by the French *Fauves* (Beasts) and by Van Gogh, Gauguin and Edvard Munch.
They undertook to express direct experience and emotion in art, in the manner
of Munch's famous painting *The Scream*. Munch described the inspiration
for this work:

> I stopped and looked out across the fjord. The sun was setting.
> The clouds were dyed red like blood. I felt a scream pass through
> nature; it seemed to me that I could hear the scream. I painted
> the picture *The Scream* from my *Frieze of Life*.[13]

This primeval scream represented the elemental forces of nature with which
the Expressionists identified. They aimed at articulating the essence of things
through an inner artistic vision.

The power of form was explored in the abstract paintings of the artists
of *Der Blaue Reiter*. This Munich-based group was established in 1911 by
the Russian-born Wassily Kandinsky and Franz Mark. They adopted a bright
blue horseman as their symbol, and were quite international and eclectic
in character. Among the well known artists from many fields who were
members were Swiss abstract painter Paul Klee and composer Arnold
Schönberg. Many Expressionists did creative work in several media: Schönberg
painted, and Klee and Kandinsky wrote poetry.

The artists belonging to this group held that art expressed spiritual truth
and form was subordinate to content (Miesel, 1970, p.45). In an essay entitled
"Creative Credo," Klee declared that "Art does not reproduce what is visible,
it makes visible" (Miesel, 1970, p.83). Kandinsky, in analyzing the nature
of artistic form, wrote:

> Form is always transient, i.e. relative, since it is nothing more
> than the necessary medium through which today's revelation can

be heard. Form is the outer expression of inner content. (Miesel, 1970, p.48)

In arguing the case for abstract art he concluded

that pure abstraction can serve things in all their corporeality as effectively as pure realism. Once again the greatest negation of objects and their greatest affirmation become identical. And this identity is the result of identical goals: the expression of the same inner sound. (Miesel, 1970, p.57)

One of the influential new forms was Cubism. Matisse invented the term in characterizing one of Braque's paintings (Laqueur, 1980, p.111). The German Expressionist painter Ludwig Meidner wrote in 1914: "But modern artists are the contemporaries of the engineer. We see beauty in straight lines and geometric forms" (Miesel, 1970, p.113). The same year Walter Gropius, in collaboration with Adolf Meyer, put these principles into practice in the architectural aesthetic of the Werkbund Exhibition buildings in Cologne.[14] Five years later Gropius established the *Staatliche Bauhaus* in Weimar.

The Expressionists' concern with aesthetics was the result of attempting to put their ground-breaking experiments on a solid theoretical foundation, and to avoid the dangers of dilettantism. This was of special concern when working in more than one medium. Many of these artists were multi-talented and advocated *Gesamtkunstwerk* or "total art", which later became the leading philosophy of the Bauhaus.

In 1912 a large exhibition of paintings was held by the Berlin *Der Sturm* group, where Expressionists exhibited together with Futurist artists. The founder of Futurism, the Italian Filippo Marinetti, read his futurist manifesto during this occasion (Allen, 1983, p.27). In this extremist document, Marinetti agitated against the European cultural past and advocated the destruction of all museums and libraries. He favored a new "mad" literary movement without any rules and restrictions (Laqueur, 1980, p.111).

Marinetti's mad vision came closest to realization in the Dada movement. This was founded in 1915 in Switzerland by a group of war refugees who gathered in Zürich in the Cabaret Voltaire. A member of the movement, Christian Schad, wrote: "Dadaism arose out of the reaction against an intellectualism which was banal because it used memory instead of reason" (Raabe, 1974, p.163).[15] Like the Futurists, they were antiestablishment and preferred chaos to control and guidelines. They delighted in outrageous proclamation and nonsensical verse exemplified by the famous first line of Hugo Ball's poem: "Gadji beri bimba." They staged absurd performances such as the racing of a typist against a sewing machine operator. Dada already reflected the anarchy of the war (Laqueur, 1980, pp.119–121).

Prewar artistic revolt was apolitical, directed against the mores of the bourgeoisie. This came most vividly alive in literature. Carl Sternheim wrote a series of plays entitled *Aus dem Bürgerlichen Heldenleben (of the Heroic Life of the Bourgeoisie)*. Thomas Mann, who was a conservative upholder of middle class tradition, was nevertheless compelled to paint a bleak picture of middle class values in his novel *Buddenbrooks* and an atmosphere of

decay and decadence in *Death in Venice,* works published before the war
(Gay, 1974, p.5).

A recurring theme in literature was the revolt against the authority of
the father. The most explicit example of this was Walter Hasenclaver's play
Der Sohn (The Son), the story of a humiliated son wishing to kill his father.
Hasenclaver's friend, the eccentric Austrian painter Oskar Kokoschka, wrote
an Expressionist play on the battle of the sexes entitled *Murderer, Hope
of Women.* After the war, from 1919 to 1924 Kokoschka held the position
of Professor of Art at the Dresden Academy (Scheyer, 1970, p.8). The young
artists of the time strove for the liberation of the individual from cultural
and ethical restrictions through inner revitalization and by focusing on the
self. It was not until the war that the artists became conscious of the need
to change society (Allen, 1983, pp.28–29).

The war came as a brutal, eye-opening shock. Artists who had been
preoccupied with aesthetics and the self, awakened to social and political
conditions. Some fought in the war, some suffered mental collapse as a result,
some turned pacifist or joined the left. They became aware of social issues
and the community, and many of them became political activists.

Franz Pfemfert's Expressionist magazine *Die Aktion* remained in
circulation during the war. It focused on the anti-war messages of a group
of pacifist artists. Free copies were sent to the front by its editor. One of
its readers in the trenches was a young soldier named Erwin Piscator (Allen,
1983, p.40). He was an actor and put on a few plays for the soldiers during
the war. Later he became world renowned for the concept he called "Epic
Theater."

Of *Die Aktion* and what it meant for soldiers at the front during the
war, Piscator wrote:

> "I set up this journal against the face of this age." When I read
> these words in the front line, when I saw the title *Aktion* before
> me, when one poem after the other gave precise poetic expression
> to my suffering, my fears, my life and my imminent death, and
> when I found myself among those real comrades for whom the
> only higher command was that of humanity, then I realized that
> no divinely ordained fate prevailed, no inevitable fate was leading
> us into this filth. It was all quite simply a crime against mankind.
> I owe this awareness to Pfemfert and his *Action*! (Raabe, 1974,
> p.182)

When the war ended a "Council of Intellectuals," made up mainly of
Expressionist artists, was formed. They met on the same day the republic
was proclaimed. Calling themselves the Novembergruppe, they issued a
manifesto in which they called for "hard tireless creative work" and for
"the moral regeneration of a young free Germany" (Friedrich, 1972, p.154).
They published their views on art in a book entitled *Ja! – Stimmen des
Arbeitsrates für Kunst in Berlin (Yes! – Voices of the Workers Council
for Art at Berlin)* (Willett, 1984, p.24). Gropius declared that "Art and state
are irreconcilable concepts." The goal of these artists was to reach the people,
the *Volk,* a somewhat idealized German concept of the masses (Friedrich,
1972, p.154).

Piscator returned from the war and established his Proletarian Theater in Berlin. This consisted of a group of semiprofessional actors who performed left-wing revolutionary plays in beer halls and other public places for working-class audiences (Friedrich, 1972, p.251). It was during these years, 1920 to 1927, that he experimented with the techniques of the "Epic Theater." In its final form as presented in Piscator's own theater, the actors played on a multi-levelled stage in front of a screen on which various images, among them newsreels, were projected.[16] Instead of acts, the plays consisted of a series of scenes (Friedrich, 1972, p.254).

Another inventor of theatrical scenery was Leopold Jessner. He became the director of the Berlin State Theater in 1919. Instead of conventional scenery he devised a single central staircase with platforms. The steps and levels were used symbolically by the actors, with the aid of lighting, to convey emotional states. This was similar in concept to Vsevelod Meyerhold's Constructivist sets in the Russian theater of the 1920's. The exchange of ideas between Russia and the west was still going on; for example, Konstantin Stanislavsky, Meyerhold's mentor, visited Berlin with his *Moscow Art Theater*.[17] Jessner, like many of his contemporaries, produced Expressionist versions of the classics (Brockett, 1974, pp.515–516; 523).

After Piscator's Proletarian Theater went bankrupt in 1921 he leased the Central Theater for a year, then eventually was appointed as Director of the *Volksbühne* (People's Theater). Changing the text into propaganda, he reshaped historical plays into controversial pro-Bolshevik proletarian dramas. He was forced to resign and in 1927 he established his own "Piscator Theater." He opened with *Hoppla, Wir Leben (Hurrah, We Live)* by the young revolutionary playwright Ernst Toller. Toller had served five years in prison for his part in the Bavarian left-wing uprising. His play reflected his own disillusionment with his former comrades, who had turned complacent bureaucrats by the time he emerged from prison. Desperately disappointed, his hero in the play commits suicide.

Another Piscator production was Jaroslav Hacek's novel *The Good Soldier Schweik*. It was adapted for the stage by Bertolt Brecht, and a cartoon film by George Grosz was projected on a screen (Schneede, 1985, p.170). The set included treadmills and a segmented stage in the best "Epic Theater" form. The play was considered "criminally blasphemous" (Friedrich, 1972, p.254). Grosz, a member of the Communist Party for a time, wrote: "I became almost rich, and Erwin got really rich, merely by making faces at the rich and mighty, and displaying our bare behinds" (Grosz, 1983, p.126).

As Piscator's star ascended, he decided to have a theater built, designed to accommodate all aspects of stagecraft. He commissioned Gropius to create the architectural design for what they together called "Total Theater." The theater was never built, but the blueprints still exist and the concept became influential in theater architecture. A description of what the theater was supposed to be like is provided in Oscar G. Brockett's *History of the Theater:*

> According to Gropius, there are only three basic stage forms — the arena, thrust, and proscenium — and in his total theater he sought to accommodate all. He mounted a segment of seats and an acting area on a large revolvable circle forward of the proscenium. When this acting area was moved to a position

contiguous with the proscenium, it formed a thrust stage, and when rotated 180 degrees it became an arena. From the wings of the proscenium stage ran an open platform which continued completely around the edge of the auditorium. It could be used as an acting area, and scenery could be shifted on it by means of wagons. A wide stage house also permitted rolling platforms to move horizontally. Spaced around the perimeter of the auditorium were twelve columns, between which could be mounted screens. A translucent cyclorama at the rear of the proscenium stage also provided a surface for projections, and other screens were mounted in the auditorium above the heads of the spectators. Gropius declared that he wished to place the audience in the midst of the action and "to force them to participate in experiencing the play." (Brockett, 1974, p.519)

Coincidentally, at this time Rudolf von Laban was searching for suitable spaces for the performance of various types of dance. In his autobiography *A Life for Dance* he lamented: "It is obvious that of all the arts it is dance that suffers most from the inability to see properly" (Laban, 1975, p.169). Later, he executed a design for the Chicago World Fair of 1933–1934 for the ideal dance theater. A sketch is to be found in his autobiography (Laban, 1975, p.186) and he gives the following description:

One of my favorite projects is a dome, flattened at the top, with the audience sitting in circular tiers of seats. The stage is in the center of the space and therefore only suitable for plastic dances, which can be looked at from all sides. In this theater all spectators are approximately the same distance from the performer. This is very important because in the usual theater buildings the subtlety of gesture gets lost as the distance increases, while those sitting in front see details of mime too clearly and at the same time do not have a full view of the whole dance area. (Laban, 1975, p.162)

Like Gropius, Laban was looking for ways to change the traditional concept of theater space, and invented unconventional methods to present a performance to the audience. His theater, like that of Gropius, was never built for lack of funds.

At least one theater project did get built, even if not from scratch. Austrian born producer Max Reinhardt remodeled a circus building in Berlin into a grand theater called *Grosses Schauspielhaus*. This theater seated over 3500 people. Besides a revolving proscenium stage, it included an arena. Reinhardt, whose reputation was established before the war, gave spectacular productions of the classics in the 1920s (Brockett, 1974, p.512). During the summers he produced plays for the Salzburg festival in Austria, among them Hugo von Hofmannsthal's widely acclaimed Expressionist play *Jedermann (Everyman)*. The characteristics of a typical Expressionist play were: a succession of scenes instead of conventional acts; characters designated by their role in life (The Father, The Son) rather than by name; grotesque and violent action, and fantasmagoric settings and costumes, all endowed with lots of symbolic meaning (Miesel, 1970, p.10).

Reinhardt also operated an acting school where the aspiring artists learned the Dalcroze method of rhythmic dance (among other subjects). One of his pupils was Maria Magdalena Dietrich, who became Marlene Dietrich, star of the world-famous film *The Blue Angel* (Friedrich, 1972, p.249). The movie was made after Heinrich Mann's well-known novel *Professor Unrat*, a scalding criticism of prewar small-town bourgeoisie.

Among the playwrights of the time, Bertolt Brecht made the greatest impact and the most lasting contribution. His poetry was well known before his first play, *Drums in the Night*, was performed in 1922 (Laqueur, 1980, p.147). He worked with Piscator on the "Epic Theater." He was a Communist who, like his friend George Grosz, was nonetheless fascinated with America, the scene of his most successful play *Mahagonny* (Laqueur, 1980, pp.33; 148). His most popular work was *The Threepenny Opera*. His musical collaborator was Kurt Weill, one of the avant-garde composers of the period.

Expressionism in music began with Richard Strauss's opera *Salome*, performed in 1905, and reached full development in Viennese composer Arnold Schönberg's atonal composition *Three Piano Pieces* in 1908 (Miesel, 1970, p.9). The new music was so controversial that Thomas Mann attributed it to the devil. He based the musical ideas of Adrian Leverkuhn, the protagonist of his novel *Doctor Faustus*, on Schönberg. The Faustian theme was a recurrent motif in German art. The first experiment leading toward atonal music was the "four triads that produce a tone row" in the *Faust Symphony* by Hungarian born Franz Liszt (Friedrich, 1972, p.178).

One of Schönberg's pupils and a master of Expressionist music was Alban Berg, the creator of the opera *Wozzeck*. The work was first performed in 1925 at the Berlin State Opera and got mixed reviews. Later critics have acknowledged it as a masterpiece (Friedrich, 1972, pp.183–184; Miesel, 1970, p.10). Other composers influenced by atonality were Stravinsky, Shostakovitch and Bartók (Laqueur, 1980, p.156).

Another kind of music, imported and spreading in popularity, was American jazz. In the 1920's American bands and musicians played in Berlin. In the dance halls jazz became the craze, while in the cabarets witty and irreverent *chansons* were sung (Laqueur, 1980, p.252). Josephine Baker became "the toast of Berlin in the 1920s," dancing nearly nude in the nightclubs (Laqueur, 1980, p.87). Meanwhile, avant-garde artists and popular entertainers met in the cafes. The best remembered was Berlin's *Romanisches Cafe* where artists, critics, singers and strippers and their entourage gathered to exchange ideas, to discuss and judge, or simply to show off their outfits or their latest companions. Berlin was the trendsetter in thought, ideas, fashion, the theater and film (Laqueur, 1980, pp. 227–228).[18]

The German movie industry centered around a film company established in 1917 called Universum Film A.G. or UFA. In 1920 it produced a landmark in the annals of Expressionism entitled *The Cabinet of Dr. Caligari*. This was a bizarre story of insanity and murder, photographed in an unsettling way to reflect the psychological instability it portrayed. The sets were ominously tilted in dizzying angles reminiscent of Expressionist art, especially of Robert Delaunay's 1911 landmark painting *The Eiffel Tower* (Barry, 1983, p.160). *Caligari* mirrored the uncertainty of the times and the general atmosphere of impending doom (Laqueur, 1980, p.234). It became widely popular and much imitated.

Director F. W. Murnau's *Nosferatu, Faust,* and *Last Laugh* were equally popular, and Murnau's *The Last Man* made a breakthrough in cinematography: it was the first film in which a continuously moving camera was used. Fritz Lang directed *Metropolis*, the utopistic sentimental horror story of a factory town of the future. Josef von Sternberg directed the UFA company's very first sound film: *The Blue Angel.* Fritz Lang's first sound film, titled *M,* was a psychological study of a compulsive child murderer. His portrayal of M made an international star out of Hungarian actor Peter Lorre (Friedrich, 1972, pp.330–331).

G. W. Pabst's *Street Without Joy* catapulted Greta Garbo into fame. Pabst also made a highly successful movie out of *The Threepenny Opera* (Friedrich, 1972, pp.322–323). As the techniques of cinematography improved, the scope of film-making widened. The subject-matter for the camera became increasingly varied. In *Berlin – the Symphony of a Big City,* made in 1927, Walter Ruttmann took the camera out of the studio and into the street, where he filmed the ordinary life of the city (Laqueur, 1980, p.241). The theme of big city life (*Grosstadt*) became increasingly popular in the arts.

The end of Germany's leadership in the film industry came in 1927 during the great inflation. To save the UFA company from folding, industrialist and Nazi propagandist Alfred Hugenberg bailed it out and took control of it. From then on, talent from the film industry flocked to Hollywood (Friedrich, 1972, p.296).

While Expressionism is often indiscriminately attached as a label to all the art of the Weimar period (see Willett's three-fold description above), by the early 1920's the Expressionist era was virtually over. A new trend had begun to take hold, and was soon given the name *Die Neue Sachlichkeit* or New Objectivity. The origin of the name is ascribed to a 1925 art exhibit at the Mannheim Museum. The museum director, Dr. G. F. Hartlaub, related the new expression to the mood of resignation and disillusionment that had overtaken the visionary, idealistic exuberance exemplified in Expressionism. The new style exhibited a coming to terms with reality, regardless of how unpleasant it might be. In a statement quoted in "The Arts" in 1931 Hartlaub said:

> Cynicism and resignation are the negative side of the "Neue Sachlichkeit"; the positive side expresses itself in the enthusiasm for immediate reality as a result of the desire to take things entirely objectively on a material basis without immediately jumping to ideal implications. This healthy disillusionment finds its clearest expression in German architecture. (Myers, 1956, p.280)

One aspect of the New Objectivity was the back to nature health movement emphasizing the community, folk dances, songs, and costumes. Rudolf von Laban, who was Ballet Master of the Mannheim National Theater at the time, enthusiastically supported this trend, which was later exploited for cynical reasons by the National Socialists.

In pictorial art, the representatives of the New Objectivity (also called "Verism") were Otto Dix, Max Beckmann and the versatile Grosz. These artists produced social criticism that took a realistic and objective view upon the world, avoiding the spiritual ecstasy and metaphysical abstractions of

Expressionism. They painted naturalistic portraits, scenes of poverty and deprivation, and shocking caricatures of the rich and mighty (Myers, 1956, pp.280–286).

Gropius and the Bauhaus exemplified a new practical and realistic attitude toward the use of architectural and living space (Myers, 1956, p.281). Gropius stated:

> The aim of the Bauhaus was to find a new and powerful working correlation of all the processes of artistic creation to culminate finally in a new cultural equilibrium of our visual environment . . . Based on the study of the biological facts of human perception, the phenomena of form and space were investigated in a spirit of unbiased curiosity, to arrive at objective means with which to relate individual creative effort to a common background. (Gropius, 1961, p.7)

Probably no single modernistic style of the Weimar period affected the future more profoundly than the Bauhaus. Today we are accustomed to sleek geometric forms and functionalism of buildings and living space, and of nearly all objects of our everyday life. But when Gropius established the Bauhaus in Weimar in 1919 he confronted a culture that was totally absorbed with the stuffy, frilly, gilded styles of the past. Architecture was patterned after medieval cathedrals; interior decoration played secessionist variations on baroque and rococo splendor. The conservative right, which included both the academic establishment and a large part of the uneducated masses, fought vigorously against the avant-garde in general, and against the ideas of the Bauhaus in particular (Laqueur, 1980, p.170).

Among the various artists who taught at the Bauhaus were Klee, Kandinsky, the American Lionel Feininger and the Hungarian László Moholy-Nagy. Practical workshops were held in all aspects of arts and crafts, such as wall painting, furniture design, weaving and metal work. (We still encounter Mies van der Rohe's "Bauhaus chair" in expensively decorated offices and waiting rooms, and his Seagram Building is a familiar part of New York's skyline.) Moholy-Nagy's experiments with modern typography have had a lasting influence in advertisement and industrial art. He was also interested in the multiple aspects of photography, among them photo-montage and photo-reportage (Wingler, 1984, pp.80; 115).

The Bauhaus was under constant severe attack from the conservative politicians of Weimar as a "hotbed of communism" headed by "Jews and foreigners." In 1925–6 the institution moved to Dessau. There Gropius was provided with the financial and political support he needed by the Socialist Mayor of the city. He was invited to design his own building, and the glass and steel structure became the landmark of the Bauhaus style. The institute's new official name became *Hochschule für Gestaltung* (Academy of Design) (Laqueur, 1980, pp.178–179).

In 1927 a somewhat similar but less well known school was founded in the city of Essen, called the *Folkwangschule*. It comprised three establishments: a museum and art collection, a school of music and the performing arts, and a school of design, arts, and crafts. Jooss was one of the co-founders of the school and became director of the Dance Division

(Markard & Markard, 1985, pp.36–37). He formed the *Folkwang Tanz Studio*, a performing body with a modest name. This group merged with the Essen Opera Ballet and became the *Folkwang Tanzbühne*.[19] This was the company for which Jooss choreographed *The Green Table* in 1932. In that same year, because of Nazi persecution, the Bauhaus moved from Dessau to Berlin. Under continuing persecution, it dissolved within the year (Gay, 1974, p.105).

Berlin was a dangerous place by then. In his autobiographical novel *Mr. Norris Changes Trains*, Christopher Isherwood writes that "The whole city lay under an epidemic of discreet, infectious fear. I could feel it like influenza in my bones" (Isherwood, 1952, p.265). Most artists left Germany; many emigrated to Switzerland, England or the United States. Jooss and his company, as we shall see, escaped in the dead of night to Holland, then moved on to England. Oskar Schlemmer, a painter and designer who had been Director of the Bauhaus theater, took refuge in Switzerland. As the choreographer of several experimental ballets, Schlemmer was an important link between avant-garde art and the German modern dance of the post-war years.

Notes

1. The armistice was not signed by anyone from the military high command, whose members shirked this odious responsibility, but by the leader of the Central Catholic Party, Mathias Erzenberg. His name also appeared on the hated Versailles Peace Treaty as Deputy Chancellor and Finance Minister. In retaliation, he was later assassinated by members of a patriotic society (Friedrich, 1972, pp.55; 82).
2. Count Kessler was an eminent personality of the time. A skilled diplomat and a capable writer, he kept careful records in a lengthy diary of the political and cultural events in which he was a participant or an observer.
3. The declaration of the Republic was nearly accidental. Interrupted while lunching on a bowl of potato soup, Scheidemann was called upon in the emergency to make a speech to the people assembled in front of the Reichstag. He did so from a window, and on the spur of the moment he spontaneously shouted: "Workers and soldiers! The cursed war is at an end . . . . The Emperor has abdicated . . . . Long live the new! Long live the German Republic!" Otto Friedrich gives an amusing account of this incident as related by Scheidemann himself (Friedrich, 1972, pp.23–24).
4. Interview with Tobi Tobias in New York on September 26, 1976. The interview was recorded for the Oral History Project for the Dance Research Collection of the Lincoln Center Museum and Library for the Performing Arts. A short section of the transcript is quoted by the Markards (Markard & Markard, 1985, pp. 48–49).
6. Hitler began dictating the meandering manuscript to his faithful aide Rudolf Hess in the summer of 1924 and finished dictating after his release from Landsberg prison. Volume one was published in 1925 and volume two in 1926. The book was generally ignored until Hitler came to power, when it became advisable for every German to own a copy (Shirer,1960 pp.80–82). It seems that it continued to be ignored by foreign politicians who preferred not to take seriously Hitler's *Weltanschauung* and his power to carry out the policies he had set forth in writing.
7. Aristide Briand was the French Foreign Minister at the time. In 1926 he and Gustav Stresemann shared the Nobel Peace Prize for their antiwar efforts (Friedrich, 1972, p.282).

8.   The famous article 48 of the Weimar Constitution authorized Presidential rule by decree in an emergency, when the welfare and safety of the people demanded it. This decree, together with the Enabling Act that put all legislative functions into the hands of the government, made it possible for Hitler to rule legally with dictatorial powers (Shirer, 1960, p.274).

9.   Oscar von Hindenburg failed to pay taxes on a large real estate transaction. Hitler threatened him with exposure unless he agreed to support Hitler's candidacy for the Chancellorship. His support was rewarded with a promotion to general and five thousand acres of land (Friedrich, 1972, p.380).

10. In 1930, three young lieutenants of the Army were courtmarshalled for inciting their fellow officers not to fight back in case of a Nazi revolt. Hitler was called as a witness, and he used his talent as an orator to turn the trial to his advantage (Shirer, 1960, pp.139–140).

11. Heidegger became Rector of the University of Freiburg for nine months at the start of the Hitler regime. He gave one notorious speech, "Role of the University in the New Reich," in which he expressed support for the German mission of "civilizing" the world (Grene, 1967, p.459). After this brief phase of political enthusiasm he resigned his position and lapsed into silence on political matters. George Steiner has written an insightful analysis of Heidegger's behavior that is quite accessible to the non-specialist (Steiner, 1979, pp.116–126).

12. Later the painter Emil Nolde, a close friend of Mary Wigman, joined the group (Howe, 1985, p.45).

13. Munch painted the *Frieze of Life* for Max Reinhardt's *Kammerspieltheater* (Myers, 1956, p.295).

14. Gropius collaborated with Adolf Meyer in 1911 on his first project, the Fagus Shoe Last Factory. This building and the exhibition buildings were the forerunners of the Bauhaus style (Gay, 1974, p.6).

15. In the same essay, entitled *Zürich/Geneva: Dada,* Schad records these recollections: I often took a stroll there [Bahnhofstrasse] with Arp, deep in extremely Dadaistic conversation, and it was through him that I met Laban and Mary Wigman, who afterwards visited my studio in order to dabble in graphic-rhythmic experiments; I must admit I did not like them drumming and dancing to Nietzsche. However, what mattered more to us than the primitive writhing of their beautiful souls was some form of dynamic action against the boring repetitiveness in art and disgust at the deep-rooted, senile tradition. (Raabe, 1974, p.163)

16. The Piscator Theater was located in Berlin's Nollendorfplatz, the setting for Christopher Isherwood's *Berlin Stories*. The movie *I Am a Camera* was based on these stories, and later inspired the popular musical *Cabaret* (Friedrich, 1972, pp.253; 303).

17. A large group of Russian emigrés who fled the Bolshevik regime lived in Berlin in the 1920s, among them such well known artists as Boris Chaliapin and Vladimir Nabokov. Anna Pavlova passed through, and so did Isadora Duncan with her new Russian husband Sergei Essenin. Maxim Gorky and Sergei Eisenstein also visited the city (Friedrich, 1972, pp.82–83).

18. Next to Berlin, Paris was the most exciting city in Europe. The American emigré community included Hemingway, the Fitzgeralds and the Murphys. Cocteau, Satie and Picasso collaborated with Diaghilev on the Cubist ballet *Parade* already in 1917 (Steegmuller, 1970, pp.177–178).

19. Personal communication with Anna Markard: a series of conversations in November 1984 in New York City. Anna Markard holds exclusive rights to the choreographer's extant ballets and sets, and rehearses every company that performs the ballets.

CHAPTER II: THE STATE OF THE ART

Dance in Germany: External Influences

The eminent Russian dance writer and critic Andre Levinson, in a caustic but poignant review of the 1928 Essen *Congress of German Dancers*, began his assessment of the state of dance in Germany with the following anecdotal proposition. He referred to a series of travel books by the German writer Oscar Schmitz:

> The title of each of these volumes was a definition. "The Land of Reality" was the formula for France; England was "The Land Without Music." If we apply this method of concise and striking labels to the Germany of the beginning of the century, we might name it "The Land Without Dance." (Levinson, 1929, p.144)

According to Levinson, ballet thrived in many of the capitals of Europe but declined once "transplanted to German soil and nursed in the hothouses of the Court theaters."

Nevertheless, even Levinson admitted that during the Weimar Republic the country experienced a flurry of dance activity. "The modern dance has become a national institution in Germany" he wrote in 1929 (p.143). Indeed, just as in all other arts, new forms governed by new ideas emerged in dance. Historically dance may have been alien to the German temperament, but in the experimental and inventive mood that swept the country in the 1920s, theatrical dance was practically re-invented.

> The Germans became theater dancers not because they were speaking through any known theatrical genre, but because each made himself, through fanatical self-discipline and mastery of the body, a precise performing instrument worthy of an audience. German [modern] dance substituted a cult of supreme self-discipline for theatrical tradition; it put forth a philosophy of the Physical distilled until it became the Spiritual. (Kendall, 1979, p.202)

21

No native genius of the dance had emerged in Germany before the twentieth century, but the country had not been isolated from the various dance movements abroad. Representatives of both classical ballet and the early modern dance had frequently passed through Germany as ballet masters, guest choreographers and visiting performers. As early as 1760 Jean Georges Noverre was ballet master at the Court of the Duke of Württemberg at Stuttgart. He remained for eight years in this position and produced 14 ballets for the duke's stage (Noverre, 1966, pp. viii–ix). In 1824 the romantic ballerina Marie Taglioni made her debut in the company that her father, Philippe, was directing in Stuttgart. A year later her brother Paul followed in her footsteps. He eventually married a German dancer, Amelie Galster, and settled in Berlin (Moore, 1938, pp.79; 89).

In 1908 Anna Pavlova included Berlin in her first Baltic tour. The following year she appeared in Germany again, and created a stir in the role of *Giselle* (Money, 1982, pp.77; 81). Germany became a regular part of her touring circuit, and the beginning of World War I happened to catch her in Berlin, where she was briefly arrested as a Russian national. Her signature piece *The Dying Swan* became a favorite with German audiences, and she performed it in numerous German cities. Following her premature death in 1931, Berlin mourned her at a special matinee at the State Opera, with speeches by such celebrities as Heinrich Mann and Rudolf von Laban, and performances by several dance companies (Koegler, 1974, p.23).

Diaghilev's *Ballets Russes* made its first appearance in the Prussian capital in 1910. The highlight of the program was Michel Fokine's *Carnival* (Buckle, 1971, p.132). Two years later Nijinsky dazzled audiences in Dresden, dancing the lead role of that same ballet. According to Russian dance historian Vera Krasovskaya, Diaghilev and Nijinsky mysteriously disappeared from Dresden each day:

> Even the omnipresent Grigoriev did not know that they were visiting Hellerau, where the Dalcroze eurhythmics school was located. That was why the trip to Dresden had been organized. At first Nijinsky did not respond to the exercises being done by the pupils of Emile Jaques Dalcroze, exercises that were supposed to transmit the design of a musical accompaniment to plastic movement. But little by little he began to respond to the instructions by just moving his fingers and head. (Krasovskaya, 1979, p.194)

During those visits to the Dalcroze school, Nijinsky could have encountered a serious dark-haired student named either Marie Wiegmann or Mary Wigman: it is not known exactly when she changed her name (Howe, 1985, pp.43–45). In a few years she would emerge as a pioneer of German modern dance.

Dalcroze was a Viennese-born music teacher, composer and critic. His youth was spent in Switzerland, and as a young man he moved to Germany at the invitation of a pair of admiring and wealthy brothers. In 1910 they built a school for him in Hellerau, a bucolic suburb of Dresden. It was named the Institute of Applied Rhythm, and there Dalcroze perfected and taught the movement method he named *Eurythmics*.[1] It was based on a variety of physical exercises designed to increase the pupil's awareness of the connection between musical rhythm and bodily movement. The main intention was to awaken a sense of motor instinct through correct timing and rhythmic patterns (Dutoit, 1971, p.20). He invented a set of balanced gestures that "were most sensibly applicable to the science and craft of theatrical dancing, particularly in relation to choreography" (Kirstein, 1977, p.286).[2] These disciplined exercises greatly influenced the development of German modern dance.

A less direct, more subtle influence on German dance was exerted by early American modern dance. This carried the mark of Francois Delsarte (1811–1871), a remarkable Frenchman who formulated a set of "laws of expression" (Shawn, 1963, p.15). His system of exercises was based on gestural communication. It reached the American continent in the form of "Harmonic Gymnastics," where it had a formative influence on all the early American modern dance pioneers. Ted Shawn writes:

> Isadora Duncan was born in 1878, Ruth St. Denis was born in 1880, and I was born in 1891 – so it was during the childhood of all three of us that Delsarte reigned supreme in America in all the fields having to do with expression through the human body. (Shawn, 1963, p.80)

While Dalcroze's inspiration came from music, Delsarte's came from acting and pantomime. All three of these dimensions of stagecraft are intimately related to dance.[3] The discovery of an inner bodily rhythm and the search for meaningful, expressive gesture were fundamental aspects of modern dance. To this Laban added the detailed analysis of the dynamics of bodily movement in space. These three brilliant visionaries, theoreticians and educators laid the foundations of all that is considered modern dance today.

Dance critic Elizabeth Kendall accurately states that Mary Wigman's dance "can be seen as the final flowering of Francois Delsarte's dream of exact spiritual and physical equivalents" (1979, p.203). She suggests a direct line of succession from Delsarte to Laban. The succession exists, though not exactly in the form she describes:

> There is a traceable succession from Delsarte down through German dance: Dalcroze, who taught Laban, who in turn taught Wigman, did indeed borrow large chunks of Delsarte for his movement theories (a famous Delsarte professor was teaching in Vienna while Dalcroze was studying music there around 1906). (Kendall, 1979, p.203)[4]

The fact is that Laban never studied with Dalcroze. His approach to movement was based on the relationship of the body to space and dynamics. he was inspired by emotion unlike Dalcroze, whose source of inspiration for movement was music. Laban did take lessons in movement from a pupil of Delsarte in Paris, a Monsieur Morel (Maletic, 1987, p.5). For her part, Wigman studied both with Dalcroze and with Laban. Instead of speaking of "borrowing," it would be more accurate to say that each of these geniuses built upon the inventions of his predecessors.

Lois Fuller, the first American modern dancer to reach Europe, was naively unaware of all art and movement theory. She was the spectacular skirt dancer who had begun her career in the Casino Theater in New York in 1891 and moved on to the Folies Bergères in Paris. While in Europe she visited Germany and was favorably received in the solo spectaculars in which she used voluminous, swirling, illuminated material for costumes (McDonagh, 1976, p.20).

Next came Isadora Duncan, dressed in simple chiffon material that she draped around herself in the imagined manner of the ancient Greeks. She danced in a new, free, deeply felt personal style. In 1902 her appearances in Munich, the cultural center of Germany at the time, were a sensational success (Seroff, 1971, p.62). During the following year she danced at the Berlin Opera House. It was in Germany that she met the actor and revolutionary stage designer Gordon Craig, who became the father of her first child (Steegmuller, 1974, p.23).

Duncan was the inspiration of artists, poets, aspiring concert dancers and feminist dress reformers. While in Berlin in 1904 she founded the first of her many schools for children. Her tours took her all over Europe but she returned to perform in most of the major cities in Germany. At the world-famous music festival of *Bayreuth* she danced the Bacchanale in Tannhäuser at the invitation of the composer's widow, Cosima Wagner (Seroff, 1971, p.72). Years later, in the summer of 1930, Kurt Jooss and Rudolf von Laban jointly choreographed that Bacchanale for seventy dancers in a grand production under the artistic supervision of Siegfried Wagner and the musical direction of Arturo Toscanini (Laban, 1975, p.173; Markard & Markard, 1985, p.41).

On the heels of Isadora, Ruth St. Denis performed her Oriental dances in 1906 in Berlin. On one occasion, while she was still in her dressing room, she survived an amusing incident of theatrical censorship. Her diary recounts:

> Well, the morals of the German public are preserved . . . . The "government" preceded by Braff [her future agent] came to inspect my waistline! I turned and twisted, evidently to their satisfaction, since I may continue to paint my tummy! (Quoted in Shelton, 1981, p.75)

No less a personage than Count Kessler, who was a patron of the arts as well as a political observer, feted her after a performance in Charlottenburg. German audiences were highly receptive to St. Denis's spiritual sensuality in such exotic dances as *Rhada, Incense* and *Cobras* (Shelton, 1981, pp.67–70).

Ted Shawn made his solo debut in Berlin in 1930. There he met Margarethe Wallmann, director of the Berlin branch of the Wigman School. Wigman herself taught at her original school in Dresden. Shawn was invited by Wallmann to take the lead role in her *Orpheus-Dionysus*, prepared for the Third German Dance Congress in Munich. The Congress lasted seven days and well over a thousand artists from all over Europe participated. In addition to Shawn, two other American dancers performed: Ernestine Day and Hans Wiener. "Never before had there been such a range of dance performances in Germany" (Koegler, 1974, p.19).

The Congress was dedicated to group dance, and quite a bit of factionalism existed between the groups. Shawn describes the events at the Congress in his memoirs:

> We found only two of the Congress programs at all pleasing; most of the groups danced with movements that were stark, ugly, and grotesque. Our own rehearsals made it impossible for us to go to many of the Congress discussion sessions where critic assailed critic and choreographers and dancers violently abused each other. We missed the most dramatic session during which one man attacked an artistic enemy with a straight razor, with which he then tried to commit suicide. (Shawn, 1979, p.225)

Shawn's solo performances in Berlin, Munich, Düsseldorf and Cologne were received so favorably that he was invited back the following year. While he confessed that German modern dancing had no message for him personally, he invited Margarethe Wallmann to teach Wigman Technique at the Denishawn school in California. The Denishawn principles included "dedication to every form of dance" (Shawn, 1979, p.221).

Although dance history wasn't being made in Germany at the beginning of the 20th century, it is evident that German artists and audiences were familiar with the great reformers, theoreticians and artists of modern dance. In the world of ballet, the great innovators had been Jean Georges Noverre and Michel Fokine. Each in his own time had rescued the ballet from aesthetic dead ends. Noverre did away with masks in favor of the dancers' own expressive faces, and lightened the restrictive heavy costumes. In his concept of the *ballet d'action* he argued for the unity of action, plot, pantomime and dance. Going one step further, Fokine argued for dramatic expression of each choreographic gesture, each movement of the whole body. He maintained that the classical vocabulary should be used semiotically, that movement should be developed as a sign for expression. Both Noverre and Fokine pursued the reform of ballet from within the classical tradition (Cohen, 1975, pp.58; 102).

Diaghilev brought to Germany not only Fokine's ballet but also the greatist male dancer of all time, Vaslav Nijinsky. Nijinsky's charismatic stage presence, the incredible chameleon-like personality changes with which he molded himself to each roll, and his phenomenal technical ability changed the concept of the male dancer forever. Rather than serving merely to support the ballerina, the male dancer became a focus of attention that could command equal respect. Extraordinary as a performer, Nijinsky was equally unique in his choreography, shocking and astonishing contemporary audiences with unprecedented ways of using ballet technique and musical rhythms.

Pavlova and Nijinsky were the outstanding representatives of the classical technique that reached its peak in the Russian Imperial Ballet of the Maryinsky Theater under Marius Petipa. Duncan, St. Denis and Shawn brought in the modern dance movement from the United States. Meanwhile the theories of Delsarte, Dalcroze and Laban were preparing the ground in Germany for an indigenous dance movement. By the dawn of the Weimar period a foundation had been laid for the ensuing dance explosion.

The Beginnings of a German Dance Tradition

In an article entitled "The Aesthetic and Political Origins of European Modern Dance," critic George Jackson writes:

> A lot went on in late nineteenth-century opera house productions, especially in central Europe, that was not classical dancing. The "noble" technique was used with discrimination for a very few roles or in a very few scenes. The rest of the action was carried by character dancers, mimes, marchers. (Jackson, 1985, p.47)

It is important to remember that the beginnings of the German dance movement were not guided exclusively by foreign influences. A delightfully lighthearted yet deeply insightful dramatic essay by the German poet and writer Heinrich Von Kleist provides an important illustration.

The protagonist is a performer, employed as principal dancer at the opera. He is fascinated by the entertainment of the crowd in the marketplace and carries on a Socratic dialogue with the narrator on the educational value of the puppet theater for the dancer. The title of the story is "Über das Marionettentheater". It was first published in 1810.[5] The dialogue illuminates many fundamental problems of dance aesthetics through the analysis of the movements of a marionette. This is especially relevant to German dance, because a century later some of the same problems intrigued Bauhaus choreographer Oskar Schlemmer.

Kleist conveyed the true nature of the art of dance through a few pointed observations on the movements of a puppet:

> Each puppet, he said, has a focal point in movement, a center of gravity, and when this center is moved, the limbs follow without any additional handling. Every time the center of gravity is guided in a straight line, the limbs describe curves that complement and extend the basically simple movement. The puppet would never slip into affectation (if we think of affectation as appearing when the center of intention of a movement is separated from the center of gravity of the movement). The force that pulls them into the air is more powerful than that which shackles them to the earth. It is simply impossible for a human being to reach the grace of the jointed doll. (Kleist, 1955, pp.386–388)

It might seem paradoxical to maintain that the movement of a mechanical doll is superior to the natural movements of a human body, but as an allegory[6] the statement illuminates nearly all the essential elements of dance: balance, harmony, gestural motivation, elevation and grace. The discovery of the body's center of gravity accounts for balance. The origin of movement lies at this center, as does the impetus for the movement of the limbs. This in turn makes for harmonious motion and meaningful gesture. The classical dancer disguises the force of gravity to give the illusion of flight and an image of grace. Kleist's poetic analogy of puppet and dancer exhibits remarkable insight into the mechanics and aesthetics of the human body in motion.

The conceptual pioneers of 20th century German dance were Oskar Schlemmer and Rudolf von Laban. Schlemmer's experiments and proposals for the field of dance derive from his deep immersion in the spirit of the Bauhaus movement. His ideas will be sketched first, although both he and Laban were active throughout the Weimar years. Laban's conceptions had a profound influence on the German dance tradition, especially as transmitted through the dance theater of Kurt Jooss, and they will be explored at greater length in the next section. Schlemmer's influence upon subsequent German dance was negligible in comparison with Laban's.

The problem that fired Schlemmer's imagination was the relationship of the human figure to space. His choreography merged the mechanical with the human. The dancer's body was rounded with padding into a uniform shape, and took possession of the space around it. The puppet came to life; the static became dynamic. This approach becomes more understandable when one remembers that Schlemmer came to dance through pictorial art. His conscientiously kept diary contains this entry for September 7, 1931:

> I readily concede that I came to the dance from painting and sculpture; I appreciate its essential element, movement, all the more because the expressive range of the former two arts is restricted to the static, to the rigid, to "movement captured in a fixed moment." (Schlemmer, 1972, p.283)

Schlemmer was trained as an artist at the Stuttgart *Academie der bildenden Künste* (Academy of the Plastic Arts). At the age of 24 he had a horizontal bar suspended from the ceiling of his room to prepare his body with gymnastic exercises for the strenuous activity of dance (Scheyer, 1970, p.30). By then he had a "vision" not only for a dance, but for a new dance style which he conceived as a bridge between the classical and the avant-garde. His December 20, 1912 diary entry begins with the sentence: "Development from the old dance to the new" (Schlemmer, 1972, pp.7—8).

His first ballet scenario, according to the same diary entry, was very much influenced by the Russian Ballet. He never did create the piece, but its description foreshadows the important elements of his subsequent ballets, especially his symbolic uses of color and masks. A demon has a "provocative yellow-orange color" and wears a mask; a violet dot, created through lighting effects, widens into a circle and passes over and into a blue square; an angel appears in shining silver. The emotional values assigned to colors were reminiscent of the spiritual qualities that the Expressionists Kandinsky and Klee gave to color and to form. For example, orange or lemon yellow symbolized "morbid overstimulation, ecstasy" (Schlemmer, 1972, p.8).

The experiments in which he disguised the human figure in costumes and masks were more like the artist's play with form than like the choreographer's search for movement expression. He turned his dancer into a generic representative of man, a *Kunstfigur* or "art figure" (Manning, 1985, p.12). Nevertheless he maintained that his interest lay not in abstraction, nor in the mechanical, but in the human. "Not machine, not abstract — always man!" he exclaimed in his diary (Schlemmer, 1972, p.116). In his well-known essay on the Bauhaus theater he suggested that von Kleist had tried to substitute the marionette for the human organism in order to "free man from his physical bondage and to heighten his freedom of movement beyond his native potential" (Gropius, 1961, p.28). In his own choreography for the theater of the Bauhaus he explored the universal human figure, disguised in costume and mask and moving through a timeless space (Gropius, 1961, p.8).

Schlemmer was invited to join the Bauhaus staff in 1921. He was placed in charge of the sculpture workshop which he soon enlarged in scope to include a stage workshop (Gropius, 1961, p.7). His talents included the design of scenery and costumes and the painting of murals. He created the costumes and decor for the Stuttgart production of Oskar Kokoschka's outrageous play *Murder, Hope of Women* (Scheyer, 1970, p.32). His murals and reliefs decorated the stairwell of the Bauhaus building and were considered the embodiment of the unity of art and architecture, the principal aim of the Bauhaus (Wingler, 1984, p.64).[7] Schlemmer's own goal was the *Gesamtkunstwerk* or total work of art, unifying music, movement and the visual arts (Scheyer, 1970, p.29).

Although Schlemmer remained first and foremost a painter, he choreographed a variety of works of which the best known is the *Triadic Ballet*.[8] According to dance critic Jack Anderson, Schlemmer first created the elaborate tubular, spiral or disk-like costumes, then choreographed the movement to fit them (Anderson, 1986b). The ballet was obviously experimental and as such it appealed to the intellectuals of the time. It was so successful that he won a prize with it, in 1932, at the International Dance Congress' choreographic competition in Paris. This was the same well known competition where Jooss won first prize with *The Green Table*. German choreographers Rosalia Chladek and Dorothea Gunther also won the second and third prizes respectively (Koegler, 1974, p.27). Schlemmer's work was awarded sixth place among the twenty competing entries (Schlemmer, 1972, p.296).

The *Triadic Ballet* consisted of three parts that progressed from the burlesque through the ceremonious to the mystical. Each part had its corresponding color scheme: yellow, pink and black. The costumes consisted of padded clothing and stiff forms made of papier-mache and coated with color or metallic paint. These devices were virtual trademarks of Schlemmer's design (Gropius, 1961, p.34). Another noted work by Schlemmer is the "Figural Cabinet" which he described as "half shooting gallery, half metaphysical abstractum." From the images cited one gets the impression of a pantomimic theater piece, "a variety of sense and nonsense, methodized by Color, Form, Nature, and Art: Man and Machine, Acoustics and Mechanics" (Gropius, 1961, p.40).

The works with which we are most familiar today are his "Dances for the Experimental Stage," created for the Bauhaus at Dessau in 1926 (Scheyer, p.43).[9] Starting with *Figure in Space*, Schlemmer placed the human form within the abstract geometry of the stage. In *Space Dance* he explored movement in different tempos; in *Form Dance*, the basic forms of circle and line. In *Gesture Dance* and *Block Party*, the masked and padded figures came alive to mock social conventions and authority. The idea of *Hoop Dance* and *Pole Dance* seemed to be to lift the two-dimensional circle and line off the artist's drawing board and to create three-dimensional images through the interplay of lighting and motion.

All of these dances were experimental in nature and explored basic movement concepts. In a way, Schlemmer reinvented the dance for himself, as if it had never existed before. He did this through the graphic arts by animating pictorial and sculptural images. For this reason his choreography was artistically one-dimensional. He remained a dedicated amateur of the dance whose real genius lay in painting.

Except for the obligatory opera ballets, Germany lacked a well-developed dance tradition. It is not surprising that the avant-garde turned toward other sources for the discovery of new movement principles and means of expression. Schlemmer arrived at dance through pictorial art, Dalcroze and his pupils through music, and Laban (as we shall see) through mystical formulations of the harmonic laws of the universe. Other artists, teachers and visionaries arrived at dance movement through physically and spiritually disciplined body-culture, using rhythmic and gymnastic exercises as training (Koegler, 1974, p.4). A contemporary observed that

> The methods of physical culture, in fact, play a great part in the formation of the modern dancer. Many of the artists directing these groups of sinewy virgins are diploma'd monitors, gymnarsiarchs promoted to choreography. The exercises of Frau Doktor Mensendieck of Vienna have inspired more than one dance-cult. (Levinson, 1929, p.147)

Bess Mensendieck and Rudolf Bode initiated new forms of gymnastics that were oriented toward body culture rather than competitive sports (Maletic, 1987, p.36).

The Dalcroze school in Hellerau produced quite a few dancers with real potential. Foremost among them was Mary Wigman, who became one of the leading artists of her day. Hanya Holm, Valeria Kratina, and Rosalia Chladek were also trained there. They were "recital dancers" (*Podiumstänzerinnen*) who specialized in solo concerts (Koegler, 1974, p.4).

In 1913, after leaving Hellerau, Wigman joined Laban's summer school in Ascona on Lago Maggiore in Switzerland, and soon became his assistant (Howe, 1985, p.46). Laban called this dance collective his "dance-farm" not only because of its outdoor classes and natural living, but also because the focus of all activity on the farm was dance (Laban, 1975, p.85). Wigman eventually forged her own method of teaching, and in 1920 she opened her own school at Dresden. Here she trained dancers of the caliber of Yvonne Georgi, Gret Palucca, Margarethe Wallmann, Max Terpis, and Harald Kreutzberg (Koegler, 1974, p.4).

Wigman herself was above all a performer. She and Laban were the originators of the German *Ausdruckstanz* or expressive dance.[10] Wigman's biographer Hedwig Muller writes:

> The word *Ausdruckstanz* is not a label for a single dance ideology or theory with clearly defined technique and teaching method. Rather it is a collective term for some highly contradictory dance

concepts, ranging from the truly expressionist to those making
political statements. (Markard & Markard, 1985, p.13)

For example, one of the more impressive dancers of the period was Hans
Weidt, a self-proclaimed communist. He actively sought to change society:
"To bring this change into effect through my art, I did not want to be a
mirror but a flame" (Scheyer, 1970, p. 24).

Ausdruckstanz is not to be confused with Expressionist dance, although
both Laban and Wigman were involved in the Expressionist movement.
Wigman was a personal friend of the artist Emil Nolde, and during her student
days she even modelled for him to make ends meet (Howe, 1985, pp.44–45).
In her correspondence with Scheyer she wrote:

> Years later at my dance showings in Berlin, Nolde always had three
> seats reserved – one for himself, one for his wife and one for
> a palette and small containers of paint. He sketched then almost
> without interruption. (Quoted in Scheyer, 1970, p.15)

In 1917, while she still worked in Switzerland with Laban, she briefly
joined the Zurich circle of Dadaists (Shelton, 1981, p.48). At this time,
resentful of the convention of subordinating dance to music, she began to
experiment with improvised percussion and even silence to accompany
movement. The most dramatic example of a dance without music is her *Witch
Dance* (*Hexentanz*), which she began to work on during her stay in Ascona.
Wigman performed it later in its final version, with mask, during her 1930
American concert tour. Critics and audiences here saw in it an expression
of the political and social turmoil of post-war Germany (Scheyer, 1970,
pp.11; 15).

Wigman gave her first solo concert in 1919 in Davos, Switzerland. She
had choreographed the dances while recovering from the nervous breakdown
she had suffered a year earlier. Her concert was attended by patients of
the *Kurhaus*: winter sportsmen, war victims and a gathering of the usual
idle misfits, gamblers and fortune hunters attracted to winter resorts.
Nevertheless, this group formed an appreciative audience, unlike the Berlin,
Munich and Hamburg public who saw her dance later the same year (Howe,
1985, pp.50–52).

Soon she founded a company of twenty women from the students at
her Dresden school (Manning, 1987, p.12). They performed *Celebration* (*Die
Feier*) at the 1928 Essen Dance Congress. One of the organizers of this
Congress was Kurt Jooss, who was by this time the Director of the Dance
Division of Essen's *Folkwangschule* and of his own dance company. In his
opening speech he favored the inclusion of classical ballet technique in the
dancer's education. It was also at this Congress that Rudolf von Laban first
made public his system of dance notation. The lecture that Wigman gave
at the Congress on the new "art dance" became the basis for her book,
The Language of Dance.

By this time Wigman had gained wide acceptance in Germany. The critic
Andre Levinson acknowledged her popularity, though he was intensely
unsympathetic to her work. He wrote of *Celebration*:

Opinion has been practically unanimous in Germany in praise of
these *Rites* [sic], this liturgical, triumphant and funereal
composition of the lady whom her countrymen delight to name
"our Wigman." Savage and convulsed, obsessed and obsessing,
this large, tawny woman, with her Mongolian cast of face, secures
the triumph (the last perhaps that we shall see) of the expression
of terpsichorean barbarism. (Levinson, 1929, p.152)

Levinson was typical of many balletomanes of his time. Though he achieved
a clear understanding of the principles of the new dance, he failed to
understand its implications and did not like it (Levinson, 1929, p.144).
Wigman, with contrasting objectivity, writes of the difference between the
two dance forms:

The revised mode of terpsichorean expression we designate as the
"modern dance" in contrast to the "classic dance" or the ballet
. . . . Its forms have become so refined, so sublimated to the ideal
of purity, that the artistic content was too often lost or obscured.
The great "ballet dancer" was no longer a representative of a great
inner emotion (like the musician or poet), but had become a great
virtuoso. War has changed life. Revolution and suffering tended
to destroy and shatter all the ideas of prettiness. (Wigman, 1983,
pp.306–307)

Ted Shawn, one of the pioneers of American modern dance, understood
Wigman's significance. "Mary Wigman was truly an expression of her times
in her country" (quoted in Sheyer, 1970, p.15). Wigman experimented in
dance with the same concepts the Expressionists used in the other arts during
the Weimar period. She incorporated primitive and Gothic elements in her
dances and she created abstract pieces concerned with rhythm and space
(Sheyer, 1970, pp.20; 23). In 1923 she even choreographed a dance entitled
the Shriek after the painting by Munch. Her dances expressed sorrow and
joy; she was concerned with universal emotions. "Dance," she wrote, "is
a living language which speaks of man" (Wigman, 1966, p.10).

The language of dance criticism found expression in the first German
dance magazine, *Der Tanz*. Founded by Dr. Joseph Lewitan in 1927, it
chronicled the last few years of the Weimar dance explosion. It appeared
too late to cover the First Dance Congress in Magdeburg the same year,
but from then until Lewitan's resignation in 1933, *Der Tanz* published articles
on all dance forms and reviews of the works of many individual artists
(Koegler, 1974, p.31).

In 1928, the most prosperous year of the Weimar republic, the foundation
of the first Union of Choristers and Ballet Dancers was followed by the
creation of the Association of German Dance Critics. But prosperity in the
professional dance world lasted no longer than in society at large. By 1930
unemployment among dancers was becoming common. After the 1931
performance at the Berlin State Opera memorializing Pavlova's death, the
soloists all received termination notices. By 1932 unemployment forced
dancers to perform on the streetcorners of Berlin (Koegler, 1974, pp.23; 27).

The most significant dance event of 1932 was the first international choreographic competition in Paris at the *Archives Internationales de la Dance* sponsored by Rolf de Maré. The triumph of Jooss's *Der Grüne Tisch* (*The Green Table*) and the other German prize winners as described above secured European recognition that German dance had matured into a prominent new art form. The theoretician whose ideas had been the most significant catalyst in the development of German dance had been Rudolf von Laban. His theories require detailed study, both for their general importance in German dance and because of their formative influence on Kurt Jooss.

Rudolf von Laban

A typically enthusiastic summary of the talents and accomplishments of Rudolf von Laban is given in an article written for *Dance Magazine* on the hundredth anniversary of his birth:

> He was a visionary and a prophet, a social philosopher, a choreographer in search of new directions, a teacher who brought out the best in his students, and a man of tremendous personal magnetism, gifted with a wonderful sense of humor. (Au, 1979, p. 102)[11]

It is difficult to make an objective assessment of a person as versatile and charismatic as Laban. His former students and disciples refer to him with reverential awe. Sigurd Leeder, founding member of the Jooss Ballet and lifetime collaborator on the Jooss-Leeder dance technique, writes of Laban's "unflagging enthusiasm and near hypnotic stimulation" (Leeder, 1958, p.511). Mary Wigman, in a short essay entitled *My Teacher Laban*, pays him this final tribute: "Today I would like to bend my knee before him and thank him for what he was to me and for what he gave me" (Copeland, 1983, p.305). Kurt Jooss gave this appraisal of his work:

> A dancer by birth, Rudolf von Laban has striven for a lifetime with never-tiring intensity to lift the veil from the secret laws of movement and formation in Nature and eventually found the principles of a dynamic harmony in all the manifestations of life – an encouragement and consolation for those who seek the Truth and a ceaseless well of imagination for the Artist (Jooss, 1939, p.129).

Laban's talents and interests bring him within the range of that rarity in modern times, the Renaissance Man. He had formal training in architecture and drawing at the *École des Beaux Arts* in Paris; his illustrations of his dances are highly expressive and of professional quality (Maletic, 1987, p.5).[12] His career as director, choreographer and dancer is well known and his reputation as a dance educator is legendary. The system of movement notation he invented is widely used, and his scientific research into human movement is far reaching. His writings are formidable in content, if not in volume.

Though he lacked academic training in philosophy, Laban approached aesthetics in the grand German philosophical tradition, attempting to explain the actions of man systematically in the context of his universe. Jooss wrote: "to reach his aesthetic point of view, Laban rises to the level of Ethics and Metaphysics, finding new soil there, which in turn brings forth new art" (Jooss, 1939, p.129). Thornton, who attempted to systematize Laban's philosophical thinking, admitted that

> The philosophy of Rudolf von Laban is extemely complex and his many books relating to movement scarcely do justice to his beliefs. Nowhere is there a philosophy explicitly set out and his publications in German are as difficult to elucidate as are those appearing in English. (Thornton, 1971, pp.3–4)

Nevertheless, two major components of Laban's movement theory may be distinguished: one dealing with the significance of movement and the other with the principles of movement. The first he named Eukinetics; the second, Choreutics.

Eukinetics is the exploration of "the laws of harmony within kinetic energy" (Ullmann, 1974, p.30). In a 1927/28 prospectus of the Choreographic Institute Laban, Eukinetics is simply put forward as "the practical theory of expression" (Maletic, 1987, p.97). Choreutics is the study of movement in space. It is an analysis of the pathways created by human movement and gesture in space. Laban termed these pathways, the shapes traced in space by movement, "trace forms" (Ullmann, 1974, pp.5; 8).

Eukinetics presents the theory of the expressive nature of human movement. Choreutics explores the mechanics of human motion. While these are distinct realms of investigation, for Laban they are inextricably interrelated. In his work the two converge at several crucial points. For example, his theory of Harmony is comprised of the Spatial (Choreutic) and the Rhythmic (Eukinetic) aspects of movement (Otte-Betz, 1938, p.137). While the first traces the direction of movement, the second illuminates its expressiveness. Because the principles of movement are interlocked with its significance, Laban's theory of movement forms a coherent aesthetic philosophy.

Jooss, first and foremost a man of the theater, summed up Laban's work in terms of its practical applicability:

> This new research resulted in a long series of striking revelations about the nature of human beings in particular and the whole world of dynamic forms and movements in general. The practical artistic application of these findings gave Laban his twofold aspect of the New Dance: Choreutics and Eukinetics. In Choreutics he gave us the starting-point from which to understand and apply the life and vital meaning of the various directions in space. If Choreutics deals with the spatial aspect of dancing, the subject of Eukinetics is the plastic rhythm in which these movements are performed . . . . Eukinetics today provides a fascinating experience in psychophysical co-ordination (Jooss, 1939, pp.129–130).

Laban himself, in his later works, gave occasional glimpses into his overall aesthetic philosophy. In *The Mastery of Movement* he touched upon the universal significance of motion in general and of human movement in particular. He alluded to the scientific, anthropological, historical, psychological and physiological perspectives of both. According to science, *motion* "is an essential of existence." Motion becomes *movement* when used purposefully by living beings. Man has an inner urge to use time and change for his own purposes. He moves in order to attain tangible or intangible goals. These goals have values of a material or a spiritual nature. Therefore, in a way, human movement is rooted in man's value system (Laban, 1975, pp.99; 106).

In art, including the theater, man looks for guidance about values. The function of the creative artist is not to give answers about what is valuable in life, but to bring to the surface the subconscious human strivings for value and to show how they affect individual and collective lives. Laban declared that

> The value of the theater consists not in proclaiming rules for human behavior, but in its ability to awaken, through this mirroring of life, personal responsibility and freedom of action. (Laban, 1975, p.108)

He called that part of man's inner being wherein the world of ideas and values resides "the world of silence." Out of this inner world of silence emerge messages and communications to the outside world. Movement springs from this silent world as symbolic action. Man's symbolic actions come from his inner need to express more than he can convey through words. Movement is often more eloquent than words because of its brevity in comparison to verbal description (Laban, 1975, pp.95–96).

The fine distinctions in behavior that arise from man's inner being are exhibited through movement. These behavioral differences are the basis for non-verbal drama such as dance and mime. A "theatrical performance" is a series of carefully selected and ordered movements and events. It is a composition constructed to evoke a mood, a state of mind in the spectator which makes him aware of "some particular aspect of the significance of life" (Laban, 1975, pp.112; 160).

The actor-dancer in a character portrayal has to mirror the inner disposition of the person he depicts. Depending on the character, on the qualities and values for which he strives, the portrayal will require different shapings of gesture in space, patterns of locomotion and the carriage of the body. The actor-dancer must be conscious of even the smallest movements: the wrinkling of a nose, the slight lifting of a chin. These movements reveal a person's inner processes; when produced unconsciously they may betray his conscious statement. Laban calls them "shadow movements"; they are the constant shadows of our consciously intended movements (Laban, 1975, pp.12; 109–110).

Just as movement arises from a person's character, so actions themselves have the power to create a mood or an inner attitude. Laban investigated the interaction between body and mind as expressed through the temporal and dynamic qualities of movement. Eukinetics is simply his term for the study of the expressive qualities of dance movement.

Laban's aesthetic philosophy was rooted in the early development of his movement theories. Jooss, as Laban's star pupil and collaborator, participated in the seminal stages of Laban's inquiries. The discoveries of this period remained influential throughout Jooss's career. This was especially true of Eukinetics, the origin of which goes back to Laban's initial attempts to analyze and classify the characteristics of movement. As Maletic points out:

> Two of his [Laban's] student-collaborators, Dussia Bereska and Kurt Jooss, were particularly instrumental in discussing and elaborating Eukinetics with the master and frequently taught the subject. (Maletic, 1987, p.98)

The origin of Eukinetics goes back to Laban's earliest attempts to think about movement analytically in an organized fashion. References to Laban's early works can be found in Vera Maletic's *Body Space Expression* (1987). Here the author traces the evolution of Laban's theory of movement. She also indicates the subsequent contributions and additions made by Laban's various associates and admirers.

The first step in Laban's classification of movement properties was the distinction between balance or equilibrium and motion, or as he referred to it *stability* and *lability*. He believed that movement also possesses the contrasting qualities of bound and released. These movement qualities gave rise to the contrasting dynamics of tension and relaxation.

According to Laban, the most fundamental quantitative movement properties were *space, time* and *force* and the qualitative ones were *fluency, flux* and *flow*. Each quantitative movement property can be used in diametrically opposite ways. The use of space can be central or narrow, and peripheral or wide; the use of time can be slow or fast; the use of force can be little or much. What gives movement its desired expressiveness and determines its *mood* is the specific combination of these movement qualities. In addition, to convey greater nuances of expressiveness Laban and Jooss used a terminology of eight movement qualities: gliding, floating, pressing, wringing, thrusting, slashing, dabbing, and flicking (Maletic, 1987, pp.93–99).

In the 1930 prospectus of the *Folkwangschule*, Jooss included both Eukinetics and Choreutics in the curriculum. They were described as "the awakening and fostering of movement phantasy and expression; the study of harmonious movement sequences and their spatial and expressive relationships" (quoted in Maletic, 1987, p.98).

Laban differentiated between two kinds of space: the space around the body, and the space within which the body moves in creating a path. The first he called the *kinesphere*, the second the *dynamosphere*. In Choreutics he mapped out both spatial spheres in terms of what he considered to be the laws of the harmony of movement, relating them to corresponding shapes in solid geometry (Laban, 1974, p.115).

"Empty space does not exist," wrote Laban (1974, p.3). It is only an illusion of the mind which perceives a momentary standstill in the perpetual "universal flux," a fragmented section of the continuous flow of movement.

Man moves according to the structure of his body and the laws of balance and harmony. The body itself is divided into five zones because of its bilateral symmetry: the zone of the head, the two zones of the arms and the two zones of the feet. In a wide open, second position stance, with the arms held shoulder level straight out to the sides, the body forms a pentagon. According to Laban:

> An intensive study of the relationship between the architecture of the human body and its pathways in space facilitates the finding of harmonious patterns. Knowing the rules of the harmonic relations in space we can then control and form the flux of our motivity. (Laban, 1974, p.25)

Laban began to explore the laws of human movement in his early theory of Space Harmony. His starting point was the five positions of the feet in classical dance and the three dimensions of the body: height, width and depth. He augmented this with the six special movements in fencing called parrying: they protect the vulnerable areas of the body and consequently form a natural sequence linking the limbs and the five zones of the body. These natural sequences form the basis of the development of harmonious movement (Otte-Betz, 1939, p.161).

The space around the body, criss-crossed by the pathways of movement, was called the kinesphere. The body moves in a natural sequence based on the structure of the joints. The spatial spheres of the kinesphere consist of vertical (height), lateral (width) and horizontal (depth) planes. These three planes form the cube. The movement which follows the path of the planes of the cube is *stable*. Movements which follow paths at angles to the planes are called *diagonals*, and are *labile* (Otte-Betz, 1939, p.161).

In the kinesphere the cube forms the center of the body's spatial orientation. Laban extended this geometric form into a rectangle according to the shape of the body and the six basic directional paths. In the end his modifications of the cube resulted in his famous *icosahedron*. Laban drew the conclusion that all movement is contained by the complex boundaries of this multi-faceted geometric form. Because the icosahedron is a common crystalline formation, Laban came to believe that human movement and the formation of matter were related in what he called "dynamic crystallography" (Laban, 1974, pp.101–103).

Jooss found these formulations amazingly insightful with regard to human movement, though he gave them a less metaphysical interpretation:

> At the same time he revealed a wonderful system of harmony underlying the structure of our natures, which has its clearest expression in that fascinating thing, the "Icosahedron." The interplay between the three dimensions and their four space-diagonals is clearly manifested in this twenty-sided crystal form. The "Icosahedron" is, therefore, the structural basis of all human movements or postures, and so the basis of our conception of space. (Jooss, 1939, p.129)

Laban classified dancers in three categories according to their ability to move in space. The "high dancer" is best able to move vertically in space. He is light on his feet and can jump high, defying gravity. The "low dancer" moves close to the earth; his movement is strong and impressive. The "middle dancer" moves horizontally across space in the middle levels. He is best suited for "swinging" movements (Otte-Betz, 1983, p.147).

The pathway of the dancer's movement creates shapes in space which Laban called "trace-forms." He classified them in four categories, relying on the French choreographer Feuillet's description of the four ways of executing classical ballet steps: straight (*droit*), open in an inward or outward arc (*ouvert*), circular (*rond*), and wavy (*tortillé*). These floor and air patterns are further emphasized by their direction in space and by the way the body of the dancer is held. The body position can be linear or one-dimensional, plane-like or two-dimensional, and plastic or three-dimensional. As Laban points out in his book *Choreographie*:

> The essential is whether the *directions* are dimensionally or diagonally emphasized, then the *path* into which these directions face, such as round, spiral, straight, and perhaps also the way in which the body holds its *equilibrium*, for which the limbs are used. (Quoted in Maletic, 1987, p.64)

Jooss had first-hand knowledge and understanding of Laban's movement theories. As Laban's pupil and collaborator, he was personally involved in developing and testing them. As early as 1920 Jooss joined a group of Laban's students in Stuttgart, and by 1922 he became Laban's chief assistant and one of the lead dancers in the *Tanzbühne Laban*. According to A. V. Coton, during those early days Jooss was "one of the dancer models whom Laban used for his research" (Coton, 1946, p.16). In his autobiographical essay Jooss writes: "I was a student, dancer, and later regisseur with Laban in Mannheim, Stuttgart, and Hamburg" (Markard, 1982, p.18).

Laban's theories at this point were somewhat ambiguous. These were formative years for him, for Jooss and for German modern dance itself. It was a period of trial and error. Laban was both inspired and inspirational and when Jooss himself began to choreograph, quite early in his career, he started to implement many of Laban's theories on the stage. He began creating his own mode of dance expression but he relied upon Laban's principles of Choreutics and Eukinetics (Coton, 1946, p. 26; Markard & Markard, 1985, p.147). The technique he used was a unique grafting of the principles of modern dance onto some of the basic disciplines of classical ballet. The movement he invented expressed the nature of the characters he intended to portray in his dances. It depicted their actions in the light of their inner motivations. In this way Jooss instinctively made creative use of Laban's intellectual concepts of movement analysis.

Jooss stayed with Laban for four years, and then set out on his own. "I needed independence for my further development, so with great regret I left the *Tanzbühne Laban*" (Markard, 1982, p.18). The break was natural for a young creative artist at the beginning of his career, but it did not occur entirely without difficulty.[13] Laban initially resented Jooss's departure. This was understandable, since he lost his star pupil and a valuable source of help. The friendship between the two men became strained for a while. Jooss's full-length ballet *Tragödie* (1926) was inspired by this autobiographical episode (Häger, in press).

Jooss's break with Laban did not lead to a significant difference of artistic opinions. The high regard in which the two men continued to hold each other was evident from their public statements. "You are a poet who can give utterance to the eternal ideas of humanity as well as the problems of our own day in the language of an entirely new art," said Laban of Jooss (Storey, 1940, p.596). In a 1928 essay, Jooss wrote of Laban:

> His importance lies far beyond all conflicts about his person or his artistic works which are available to only a very few. Laban's importance is in the founding of a new art form in Western dance. He is the founder of the modern concept of harmony in choreography, which carries within the possibilities for expansion, which will be the scaffolding of all dance forms in the future. (Jooss, 1928, p.216)

A final indication of their comfortable relationship is that when the *Zentralschule Laban* (Central School of Laban) merged in 1929 with the Dance Division of the *Folkwangschule* under Jooss's direction, Laban was appointed as the "master examiner" (*Prüfungsmeister*) of the institution.[14]

After leaving Laban's company, Jooss and his friend and colleague Sigurd Leeder established a method of dance training that was more systematic and rigorous than anything that existed in German modern dance at the time. Their technique was partially based on Laban's movement principles. Jooss writes:

> We saw the greatest need for the New Dance to be a firmly consolidated system of teaching, and we decided to abandon all other wishes and work solely to this purpose. Laban's movement teachings and his choreographic principles, combined with the discipline of traditional ballet, were to make up our materials. (Markard, 1982, p.19)

Much later, in a 1956 proposal for the establishment of a German Dance Academy, he drafted a detailed plan for dance education. In classical dance he advocated the Cecchetti Method, and in modern dance he proposed the study of "dynamic technique, tension and release, impulse and swing, stable and labile control of space (choreutics), theory, practice and technique of movement expression (eukinetics)" (Markard & Markard, 1985, p.153).

It is evident that the extent of Laban's influence on Jooss's work is far reaching. It encompasses all areas of dance: technique, choreography, and training. Although Jooss referred to Laban all through his life as his "master," from the beginning of their association their work was a collaboration.[15] Bengt Häger sums it up accurately in the biographical essay on Jooss that he contributed to the forthcoming *International Encyclopedia of Dance*:

Laban was the brilliant begetter of ideas, the visionary, the inspirer; Jooss was the great choreographer and the logical builder of an ideology, a philosophy of dance. Much of what is now ascribed to Laban, was initiated by Jooss or proven by him to be valid in practice. (Häger, in press)

Jooss had an unusual ability to work effectively with the individuals he chose as artistic collaborators, and he had many such collaborators during his long career: his wife Aino Siimola, his partner Sigurd Leeder, and the composer F. A. Cohen, to mention only a few. None of these was more significant than his collaboration with Rudolf von Laban during his early years as dancer, choreographer and teacher.

Notes

1. A somewhat similar but less accessible language of gestures called *Eurhythmy* was founded by the Austrian-born educator and mystic Dr. Rudolf Steiner (1861–1925). In 1888 he became the German leader of Madame Blavatsky's sect, known as Theosophy. Later he split with the Theosophists and founded his own philosophico-religious sect, Anthroposophy. The international headquarters of this sect, which still exists, was designed by Dr. Steiner himself and built at Dornach, Switzerland. It is known as the *Goetheanum*.
    Eurythmy is a gestural language intended to make speech and music visible. Its vocabulary links gestures with sounds of the alphabet. When combined with natural movements such as running, skipping and swaying, a dance pattern is formed.
2. Diaghilev employed Miriam Rambach to assist Nijinsky in choreographing *The Rites of Spring*. She was one of the outstanding pupils of Dalcroze. In Diaghilev's company one of her duties would have been to teach some Eurhythmic exercises, if the members had not categorically refused to learn them. Like Nijinsky she was Polish in origin, and the two of them got along quite smoothly (Kirstein, 1977, p.287). After Nijinsky's marriage she left the company and went to England where she became instrumental in shaping British ballet. She changed her name to Marie Rambert and in 1962 was made Dame of the Order of the British Empire (Chujoy, 1967, p.754).
3. Delsarte studied singing and acting at the Paris Conservatory with the aim of becoming a singer. Due to bad teaching, his voice was ruined. To prevent future students from suffering what had happened to him, he dedicated his life to the discovery of basic aesthetic principles, which he then applied in his own teaching and coaching. His research was based on practical observation of man in every emotional and physical state: in action, in suffering, and even in death. He combined his knowledge with spiritual and religious beliefs and based his system of expression on the concept of trinity and the "law of correspondence" (Shawn, 1963, pp.15–16; 27). He revolutionized acting by substituting the realistic expression of emotion for the stale and sterile pantomime practiced at the time.
4. It would take extensive comparison of the three systems to substantiate Kendall's statement, and she does not provide such documentation in her book. The scope of such a project would extend far beyond the limits of this study.
5. The essay was published in *Die Berliner Abendblätter*, December 12 and 15, 1810. Kleist was the editor of the paper (Maas, 1983, pp.226–227).

6.   Many different interpretations have been given to Kleist's essay. Many of them stress
      its metaphysical implications. Kleist's biographer writes:
      This essay, as profound as it is playful, develops an insight expressed in Kleist's
      letter to Ruhle of August 31, 1806: "Every primary involuntary movement is
      beautiful, and everything that understands itself is crooked and distorted. Oh reason!
      Wretched reason!" With these words, the central thesis of the little masterpiece
      is sketched in; for the marionette combines naturalness with lightness and with the
      unawareness which saves it from affectation − in contrast to the human dancer
      who must rest upon the ground (an undancerly feature) which the marionette barely
      grazes, and who is usually concerned with the effect he will produce, so that the
      charm of innocence is gone. (Maas, 1983, pp.226−227).
      Actually what Kleist writes is much more profound, and is expressed in aesthetic
      terms:
      The puppet would never slip into affectation (if we think of affectation as appearing
      when the center of intention of a movement is separated from the center of gravity
      of the movement).
      To illustrate his point, he continues:
      and young F − − − when, as Paris, he stands among the goddesses and presents
      the apple to Venus, his soul is (oh painful to behold) in his elbow.
      Kleist here refers to the motivating force of the movement that originates where
      the body is centered. The direction in which gravity acts on the body must pass
      through the center of gravity and the point of support. Since it is a physical
      impossibility for the center of gravity to reside in the extremities, a gesture that
      originates there necessarily remains at the periphery of the body. Such a movement
      can be decorative, but it remains superficial and devoid of true intention. In such
      instances artifice takes over the true movement impulse, and the gesture becomes
      empty and affected. Aesthetically, the gestural communication of sincerely felt
      emotion must originate from the body center, thereby involving the dancer's whole
      being.
            Kleist's emphasis on the unselfconscious innocence of the artist has sometimes
      been given a superstitious meaning. For example, the essay has been reprinted in
      a publication entitled *Universal Zen*! Nevertheless, aesthetic truths rather than
      metaphysical speculation have made the piece immortal.
7.   These works were destroyed under the Nazi regime. Schlemmer wrote to his friend
      Otto Meyer:
      In Weimar − perhaps you have read about it − is an art scandal raging because
      Frick, the National Socialist, has ordered the removal or storage of all modern art,
      and Schultze-Naumburg, Bartning's successor, has had the paintings and reliefs I
      did in 1923 painted over. (Schlemmer, 1972, p.275).
8.   The *Triadic Ballet* premiered on September 30, 1922. Schlemmer in his time was
      considered a painter rather than a choreographer or dancer (conversation with Anna
      Markard, December 7, 1987). The ballet was reconstructed in 1977 by Gerhardt
      Bohner in cooperation with the *Akademie der Kunste* of West Berlin. In New York
      City this production opened at the Joyce Theater on October 1, 1985.
9.   Debra McCall's recent reconstructions of most of these dances were performed by
      a group under her direction at The Kitchen in New York City on October 30, 1982.
      Included were *Space Dance, Form Dance, Block Play, Gesture Dance*, parts of *Hoop
      Dance*, and *Pole Dance*. In 1984, at the Guggenheim Museum, she added *Flats Dance*
      and *Metal Dance* to the program (Moynihan & Odom, 1984, pp.49−50).

10. "Ausdruckstanz" is something of a misnomer. Like American modern dance, it emerged as a dance movement that pitted itself against the classical ballet. In Hungary, for instance, this new dance form was named "movement art" (*mozdulat müvészet*). Pure self-expression has never been the aim of any art form; even the Expressionists had the higher goal of expressing mankind's universal "cry." Isadora Duncan, who was often accused of indulging in pure self-expression, actually expressed the mood of the music or a theme such as nurturing, or freedom, or the beauty of nature. Her means of expression were highly individualistic, and since she left no dance vocabulary many of her imitators could do no better than indulge in self-expression. Duncan's example is significant because she is the aesthetic originator of expressional dance.

   When it has not been in artistic decline, the classical ballet (against which the aesthetic revolt of the "expressional", "modern", or "art" dance movement occurred) has always striven for expressive, modern, artistic movement. It is true that during periods of artistic degeneration acrobatic technical feats and artless artifice became dominant, and it was against this aspect of ballet that the "moderns" revolted. In her essay on dance entitled *Virtual Powers*, Susanne Langer says:
   The almost universal confusion of self-expression with dance expression, personal emotion with balletic emotion, is easy enough to understand if one considers the involved relations that dance really has to feeling and its bodily symptoms. (Langer, 1953, p.183)

11. Rudolf von Laban was born on December 15, 1879 in the small Hungarian town of Pozsony, located on the northern bank of the Danube at the junction of what became the borders of Austria, Hungary and Czechoslovakia following World War II. The town now belongs to Czechoslovakia and bears the name of Bratislava. Laban wrote in his autobiography, "The house where I was born looked out on the same huge river on which my great-uncle had met his ignominious death" (Laban, 1975, p.6). He is referring to the Danube, next to which more than one generation of von Labans lived.

   Samuel Thornton, who wrote a book attempting to clarify Laban's movement theories, introduces him by the lengthy and somewhat dubious name of *Váraljai véreknyei és ligetfalvi Laban Rezsö Keresztelö Szent János Attila* (Thornton, 1971, p.3). The first four words refer to place names presumably connected with the Laban family title. If this were correct, the fact that Laban eventually simplified his name is perfectly understandable, especially when one takes into consideration that "Keresztelö Szent János" means John the Baptist. Unfortunately the name as given by Thornton is not documented in his book, or anywhere else in the literature. It should be regarded as merely anecdotal.

12. See also Laban's autobiography, *A Life for Dance*, which includes Laban's own illustrations.

13. Personal communication with Anna Markard, January 1985, Essen, Germany.

14. Manuscript in the Elsa Kahl Cohen Archives. Elsa Kahl Cohen is the widow of the composer F. A. Cohen and a founding member of the Folkwang Tanzbühne. She created the role of the Partisan Woman in *The Green Table*.

15. Gruen, J. Interview, March 8, 1976. Phonotape in the Dance Collection of the New York Public Library at Lincoln Center.

CHAPTER III: JOOSS THE ARTIST

The Weimar Years

Kurt Jooss lived at a crucial time in Western cultural history, a time that saw the birth of the Age of Modernism. His achievement places him in the rank of those leading artists who have permanently changed our cultural landscape. His career spanned several decades, but he came of age as a creative artist during the seminal years of the Weimar Republic.

Jooss was born on January 12, 1901 in Wasseralfingen in the Baden-Württemberg region of Germany near the historic city of Stuttgart. His family owned farm land and his father expected Jooss to inherit and manage the estate. However, Jooss himself was drawn to the arts. Instead of thinking of a career in farm management, his attention was taken up with music, drama and the visual arts. He played the piano and studied singing and drama. Because he felt that he lacked the talent to paint or to draw, he took up photography.

His father allowed him to pursue his artistic goals freely. Both of Jooss's parents had artistic talents themselves; his father was an amateur theater producer and his mother a trained singer. As a teenager Jooss also tried his hand at amateur theatricals. At the age of fourteen he created several movement improvisations, including one entitled *Salome* and another *Indian Prayer*. Instinctively Jooss searched for a medium of expression that would consolidate his talents and give him personal satisfaction.

At the age of eighteen, after graduating from the *Real-gymnasium* of Aalen, Jooss entered the Stuttgart Academy of Music. In spite of being a success at his studies, especially in acting and voice, he was dissatisfied. In an autobiographical essay he wrote:

> I studied drama devotedly and with great success but I remained
> empty. Something was missing everywhere, and I no longer believed
> in my dream of the arts. (Markard, 1985, p.29)

He was on the verge of giving up his quest for a suitable artistic expression and nearly resigned himself to a life of agricultural management when by chance he met Rudolf von Laban.[1] He had been taking lessons in movement from Grete Heid, a former Laban pupil. It was through her that

43

the two men met: a meeting that changed the course of Jooss's life and of dance history.

During the years 1920 to 1922, Laban lived and taught in Stuttgart and served as Ballet Master at the Mannheim Opera. Shortly after Jooss became his student, Laban included him in a group of twenty-five dancers whom he trained for professional performances. They appeared at the Mannheim Opera together with the Opera Ballet in Laban's own works. Jooss instantly became one of the leading dancers of this group. As Jooss modestly remembers:

> A few weeks later I danced the male lead in our first work, *Die Geblendeten* [*The Deluded*], with great success. At that time in Germany one did not need great proficiency for the "Expressionist Dance": strong intensity was all-convincing. In the meantime though I have added to my abilities. (Markard, 1982, p.18)[2]

Laban straight away recognized Jooss's exceptional ability and made him his assistant and later regisseur of his company, the *Tanzbühne Laban*. Jooss served as one of Laban's model dancers who was able to physically execute and demonstrate Laban's movement experiments (Coton, 1946, p.16). He also participated in the summer training camps in Ascona, Switzerland. Laban called it his "dance farm;" his pupils lived in a commune, close to nature, and practiced a form of minimal subsistence farming (Laban, 1875, pp.85–86). It was there, in practices held in the open air, that Jooss first participated in Laban's monumental choric works. These and other works were performed during the *Tanzbühne Laban*'s residencies in Stuttgart, Mannheim and Hamburg, and during its tours all over Germany.

While Jooss was a member of Laban's group, two important people entered his life. One was his future wife, the other a lifelong friend: both became his artistic collaborators.

In 1921, a year after Jooss's arrival, a new pupil entered the group. She had the exotic foreign name of Aino Siimola. She had been born in 1901 in the town of Narva, in Russian Estonia. This town was located inland from the Gulf of Finland, not far from the historic city of St. Petersburg. Siimola was educated in a private school that was directed by Maria Fedorovna, mother of the Russian Tzarina. Dance was one of the requirements of the curriculum.

Having chosen to become a professional dancer, Siimola decided to travel to Germany with the purpose of studying with Laban. After a short apprenticeship in Stuttgart, she became a member of the *Tanzbühne Laban*. She was a woman of great beauty and intelligence, and after she became Jooss's wife she also became his lifelong artistic collaborator.

While working with Laban in Hamburg in 1924, Jooss met a young native of that Northern city named Sigurd Leeder. Leeder studied art at the Hamburg School of Arts and Crafts. He also studied acting and took movement classes from a former student of Laban. His skills and education complemented Jooss's, and so did his looks and his temperament.

Jooss had a strong personality: he was brimming with curiosity and overflowing with abundant creative energy. Leeder was frail and finely chiselled, with a sense for form, detail and craftsmanship. The two artists complemented each other in temperament.

Jooss began choreographing early in his career, while he was still working with Laban. He created a program of short dances or *Kammertänze*, "chamber dances". Shortly after they met, Jooss and Leeder put together a program called *Two Male Dancers*. The concept of a male duo of concert dancers appearing without props or a supporting cast was new and original. The choreography was experimental, influenced greatly by Laban's theories and movement studies (Coton, 1946, p.16). The program was exceptionally well balanced, consisting of four duets and four solos for each dancer. It filled an entire evening's time. The subjects ranged from religious themes to comical parodies reflecting upon the times. It included ethnic dance and also Jazz, which was still quite new in Europe, having just recently crossed the Atlantic. Only a few photographs remain of these dances, but Jooss stands out in them for his comic talent and character sketches.

In 1924 Niedecken-Gebhart invited Jooss to join him at the Municipal Theater of Münster as "movement regisseur" and ballet master. Niedecken-Gebhart's novel approach to opera staging included the conviction that movement should be an integral part of the production. He needed a movement specialist to accomplish this goal. Jooss, who was ready to strike out on his own, accepted the position. He had achieved recognition as a choreographer and performer with a distinctive style, and he needed his independence.

Jooss then took the opportunity to establish his own company, *Die Neue Tanzbühne*. When Laban's performing group ran into financial difficulties on a Yugoslavian tour and had to disband, Jooss offered positions in his company to a few of the Laban dancers. His group was small, initially consisting of three male and four female dancers (Markard, 1982, p.18).

Die Neue Tanzbühne was technically a part of the Municipal Theater of Münster, but it was artistically independent. It was entirely under the artistic direction of Jooss. In his productions he made use of the many talented people working in the Münster Theater. Hein Heckroth created the designs for seven of the eight ballets Jooss choreographed during this period. His work contributed greatly to the unity of concept in these productions.

It was also during this time that the composer F. A. Cohen became Jooss's musical collaborator. Cohen had definite ideas about creating music for dance. He believed that the musical accompaniment should underline the dramatic meaning of the dance, accentuate the choreographic form and rhythmically aid the dancer. Jooss and Cohen shared the belief that choreography and musical composition should proceed together to give expression of the dramatic idea in unified style and form. The greatest surviving example of this collaboration is *The Green Table*. In the next few years the Municipal Theater of Münster achieved fame for its innovative productions under Niedecken-Gebhardt and the opera director Rudolf Schultz-Dornburg, and Jooss's group also became widely known in Germany.

Performances were mainly held in the Münster Theater, but the *Neue Tanzbühne* also toured throughout the country, stopping at such major cities as Berlin, Bonn, Hamburg, and Mannheim. The eight pieces Jooss choreographed during this two year period included shorter works such as *Larven* (1925), *Der Dämon* (1925), *Groteske* (1925) and *Kaschemme* (1926). Of *Groteske* he wrote:

> a tiny piece which, however, showed clearly in which direction
> my work was to develop: away from the literal, aspiring toward
> a physically and spiritually motivated dance movement and art
> form. (Markard, 1982, p.19)

Der Dämon was choreographed to music by Hindemith and it is described
as "an expressionistic ballet with symbolic figures" (Häger, p.2). The word
larve means both larva and mask in German, a double meaning which gave
a special twist to this group work. A string of crouching figures in hooded
masks and capes presented mixed images of the nature of bugs and people,
"the human insect."

The two longer pieces were entitled *Die Brautfahrt* (1925) and *Tragödie*
(1926). The libretti for both were created by Jooss. *Die Brautfahrt* was a
fairy tale in four acts, later renamed by Jooss *A Spring Tale* (1939). In this
dance Jooss once again made observations on human behavior. Jooss
considered *Tragödie* his most important work of this period, not only because
of its complexity but also because its creation was motivated by his own
personal trauma of breaking away from his mentor Rudolf von Laban. It
was a full-length ballet in four acts for four soloists and a chorus, to music
improvised by F. A. Cohen for each performance.

Meanwhile Jooss had been deeply concerned with the state of dance
education in Germany. He believed that German modern dance lacked the
kind of systematic dance training which gave classical dancers a highly
developed technique. In the spring of 1925, he and Leeder worked out a
plan for a professional dance school. He wrote:

> We saw the greatest need for the New Dance to be a firmly
> consolidated system of teaching, and we decided to abandon all
> other wishes and work solely to this purpose. Laban's movement
> teachings and choreographic space principles, combined with the
> discipline of traditional ballet, were to make up our materials.
> (Markard, 1982, p.19)

In the fall of 1925, a group of artists including Jooss and Leeder
established a new school which was named the *Westfälischen Akademie Für
Bewegung, Sprache und Musik* (Westphalian Academy of Movement, Speech
and Music). The school was under the overall direction of Rudolf Schulz-
Dornburg, who was also the music director of the Münster Theater. Jooss
was the Director of the dance division, Vilma Mönckeberg headed the division
of speech, and Hermann Erpf was in charge of the music division (Markard
& Markard, 1985, p.145). The school developed rapidly, and two years later
it moved to Essen to be incorporated into the newly-founded *Folkwangschule*.

Leeder had decided to dedicate himself to dance education. He had a
genuine interest in teaching, and concerns about his health also contributed
to his decision to change the direction of his career. He had medical problems
with his lungs. Because he seemed better during the summer vacations when
he spent much time outdoors, his doctors recommended that he not return
full time to the unhealthy, dusty air of the stage and rehearsal hall. From
then on he concentrated on dance pedagogy and became one of the most
significant European modern dance teachers. He was the greatest exponent

of the Jooss-Leeder technique of dance. His positions included that of chief instructor at the Folkwangschule (1927–1934), co-director of the Jooss-Leeder School in England (1934–1940) and ballet master of the Ballets Jooss (1942–1947) (Chujoy & Manchester, 1967, p.565).

In order to enlarge the scope of their knowledge of dance, Jooss and Leeder decided to study abroad. So far Jooss had only mastered modern dance and he felt it necessary to acquire a first-hand knowledge of classical ballet. In December 1926 the two of them went to Paris to take class with the emigré Russian ballerina Lubov Egorova. She was a graduate of the Imperial Ballet School and a principal dancer with the Maryinsky Theater, now the Kirov Ballet. She exemplified the unsurpassed tradition of a school and the purity and artistry of a technique, the representatives of which form a lineage like royalty to the present day.

In a short period of time Jooss acquired an understanding of classical ballet that convinced him of its value, importance and historical significance. He never stopped defending his view, unique at the time, that ballet and modern dance are not opposing techniques but belong on a historical continuum in the realm of dance. He believed that all available means should be used for the expression of significant human emotion. He made this clear in a statement at the International Competition of the Dance in Paris in June 1932:

> We aim therefore at discovering a choreography deriving equally from the contributions of modern art and from the classic Ballet. We find the basis of our work in the whole range of human feeling and all phases of its infinite expression; and by concentration on the "Essential" we arrive at our form in the Dance.[3]

The combined use of ballet and modern dance techniques in choreography was a completely novel position at the time. Modern dance was proclaiming its revolt against the academic restraints of ballet, and the various exponents of *Ausdruckstanz* feuded amongst themselves, each proclaiming to hold a superior point of view.

In 1926, as an addition to the program of *Two Male Dancers*, a masked dance was planned by Jooss and Leeder, tentatively called *Dance of Death*. Jooss described the plan as follows:

> We intended to work with masks, which would enable us to quickly slip into different characters (beggar, peasant woman, bishop, king, courtesan), since we were only two people. (Markard, 1982, p.18)

As a trained artist, Leeder was proficient in the design and execution of masks. He created eight sculptural likenesses of the human face, each mask with a different expression. Each depicted a particular character, who in the course of the dance would die according to the way he had lived (Coton, 1946, p.88). This was the small seed of a much greater concept that six years later came to fruition in Jooss's masterpiece, *The Green Table*.

Because of an unfortunate accident, the *Dance of Death* was never added to the program of concert dances. In January 1927 Jooss and Leeder were rehearsing in Vienna under the direction of the acclaimed theater director

Dr. Hans Niedecken-Gebhart for a performance. Gertrude Boenweiser's local school supplied the movement choir and Jooss and Leeder were to dance solos choreographed by Jooss in a scenic oratorio of Handel's *Herakles*. During one of the rehearsals Jooss leaped off a tall pedestal and wrenched his knee in landing. The performance of *Herakles*, and also a "Two Male Dancers" performance in Vienna, had to be cancelled.

Within a month he was completely disabled, and spent ten weeks off his feet recuperating from severe knee joint injury. The arthritis in his knee caused by this incident kept him in discomfort for the rest of his life.[4] Jooss remembered, with a note of dismay:

> That was the end of our touring plans and as I thought also the end of my performing career. Buried was the tour of "Two Male Dancers", buried the "Dance of Death" for which there were no performers. (Markard & Markard, 1985, p.33)

Meanwhile the Municipal Theater of Münster decided under public pressure that its artistic direction was too avant-garde. To ease the minds of the conservative municipal authorities, changes in programs and personnel were instituted. Among the people leaving were Niedecken-Gebhardt, Schulz-Dornburg, Cohen (for personal reasons) and the entire *Neue Tanzbühne*, which at this time was under the direction of one of its members, Jens Keith.[5] In early 1927 Jooss was concentrating all his efforts on a new pedagogical endeavor.

Fortunately for the *Neue Tanzbühne*, Schulz-Dornburg obtained the position of music director at the Essen Opera House and invited the entire company to join him there for the 1927–1928 season, with Keith as ballet master. In June 1927 the dance group performed two Jooss ballets, *Kashemme* and *Groteske*, at the First German Dancer's Congress at Magdeburg.

In the spring of 1927, while Jooss was in Münster recuperating from his knee injury, he began negotiations with the mayor of Essen, who wanted Jooss to direct the dance division at a new school for the visual and the performing arts. Jooss accepted the position. Together with Rudolf Schulz-Dornburg and Max Fiedler they moved the *Westfälishe Schule* to Essen, which became the core for the founding of the Folkwangschule (Markard & Markard, 1985, p.145).

In the early 1920s the city of Essen had acquired a sizable art collection named *Folkwang*.[6] In 1927 it was decided to sponsor a school of the performing arts. It was conceived as a sister school to the existing school of design, arts and crafts. The city wanted all three of its cultural institutions, the museum and the two schools, to carry the mythological name *Folkwang*. Thus, when Jooss's school was brought to Essen it became the *Folkwang Schule für Tanz, Musik und Sprechen*.

Meanwhile Jooss's knee did not get better. Hoping for a cure, he travelled to a small Hungarian town named Pistyán (now known as Piest'any and located in Czechoslovakia) known for its medicinal hot springs. He stayed for six weeks at the spa, and while his knee was being treated with mud baths he spent the time working on Laban's new dance notation. He started with the idea that movement sequences should be recorded on a vertical staff, where the right side represented the right side of the human body and the left the corresponding left side. Next he added the idea that the weight-bearing support of the body (the legs) should be represented on the middle shaft, while the arms and the head should be located on shafts further out. Jooss called this the *Linien System* (Linear System) of notation.

In the summer of 1927 Jooss and Leeder continued to work on the notation system and completed the notation of two solos, the *Courting Dance of the Princes* (*Werbetanz des Prinzen*) from Jooss's ballet *Die Brautfahrt*, and Leeder's *Maskentanz*. They attended a summer course of Laban's where they studied Eukinetics with Dussia Bereska, and took the occasion to present their developments for the notation system to Laban. Laban took up their scheme with enthusiasm and elaborated it extensively with the assistance of his disciples. This became the notation system known as Labanotation in English and as Kinetographie Laban in German. Laban acknowledged Jooss's contribution to his notation system in a preface to one of his books:

> I will mention here Kurt Jooss, who, after finishing his studies as a pupil of Bereska and myself, surprised us one day with a proposal to duplicate Feuillet's right-left division of the movement sequences. We proceeded then to record the movements of trunk and arms in separate columns instead of inserting them in the upper part of the cross mentioned beforehand.[7] (Laban, 1976, p.x)

In 1928, at the Second German Dancers Congress in Essen, Laban officially presented his notation system to the public. Critic A. V. Coton writes:

> Laban's personal efforts were eagerly taken up in his circle of disciples and collaborators, and the "Kinetographie Laban" as first published at the Dance Congress at Essen in 1928 was the result of this joint effort of which the main exponents were, besides Laban himself, Kurt Jooss, Sigurd Leeder, Albrecht Knust and Dussia Bereska. (1946, p.80)

The Congress, which was organized by Jooss, ran from June 21st to 26th. In his opening statement Jooss addressed the issue of the relationship of classical ballet to modern dance. He maintained that it was important not to lose sight of the achievements of the classical tradition, and to consider how this tradition and technique might contribute to the evolution of German modern dance. He was a lone crusader in this advocacy of combining classical and modern dance techniques. "I was nearly stoned for that," he said later, referring to the reactions of the participants to his speech (quoted in Häger, in press). Ultimately Jooss proved his point through his own choreography. It is fair to say that no choreographer in the history of dance has combined the classical and modern techniques in the service of theatrical dance drama as successfully as Jooss.

For Jooss, technique was a means for expression, choreography the form of content. By 1927, when he co-founded the Folkwangschule in Essen, he was a mature artist with a repertory of eight group works, at least four major solos, several duets and numerous dances staged and performed for operas and operettas. He had founded a school and developed a method of dance training. He was deeply committed to the theater, to professional training for dancers, and to collaborative work with other art professionals. As Häger points out:

> Laban was the dominating pace setter, Wigman the leading artist, but from the time of the Congress Jooss began to emerge as a new spiritual leader [of the dance world]. (Häger, in press)

The theme of the Second Dancers Congress at Essen was the relationship of modern dance to the traditional theater. There were differing points of view. Some, like Max Terpis, student of Wigman and ballet master of the Berlin State Opera, held that the *Podiumstänzer* (recital or concert dancer) should break free from the traditional boundaries of the theater. Wigman envisioned a utopian performing space based on the needs of movement artists. Laban together with Jooss advocated the professional theater as the place for dance as a performing art. Among this group was Yvonne Georgi, who said:

> Those who create dances for the theater must have the ability, not only to involve themselves and their own feelings in the dance, but to arrive at a *Gesamtkunstwerk* [complete work of art] by giving form and shape to their surroundings (stage-space, costumes, lighting, decor, movement) and their own expression. (Koegler, 1974, p.11)

We hear the echo of the word *Gesamtkunstwerk* from as far back in German art history as Richard Wagner. The Bauhaus was the institutionalized embodiment of the concept of "total design" in the visual arts. Jooss was probably influenced by the concept when he worked on developing the dance curriculum at the Folkwangschule. The municipality of Essen gave the following description of the school in announcing its opening:

> On Oct. 1 the City of Essen will open the Folkwang Schools, two divisions offering education in all fields of the Arts. The "School of Arts and Crafts" (*Kunstgewerbeschule*) will receive a new subtitle, "School of Form." The "School for Expressive Arts" (*Schule für Ausdruckskunst*) is conceived as a school for music, dance and speech, also including theater, art history and criticism. (Quoted in Markard & Markard, 1985, p.145)

In 1928 Jooss formed a small performing group of professional dancers and called it the Folkwang Tanztheater Studio. F. A. Cohen joined him as composer, pianist and music teacher. Out of the seven major works Jooss created for this group, the only surviving ballet is a short piece entitled *Pavane on the Death of an Infanta*. Jooss choreographed it as a fiftieth birthday present for Rudolf von Laban.[8] The ballet was premiered in October 1929 at the Folkwang Museum in Essen.

A Court Dance

The choreography of *Pavane on the Death of an Infanta* is concise in statement and style. The ballet is set in the stark and forbidding formality of a highly ceremonious court dance. The subject matter conveys both a personal and a universal message. It communicates the fundamental significance of the freedom of the spirit.

In addition to making a personal statement, Jooss drew inspiration for the ballet from Maurice Ravel's piano work bearing the same title.[9] Diego Velazquez's painting, *The Maids of Honor*, conveys a reference to the historical period through colors, shapes and atmosphere. The Velazquez painting depicts the Infanta Margaret and the Court of the Spanish king, Philip IV. A fascinating description of the painting is given by historian Martin A. S. Hume in his book entitled *The court of Philip IV*:

> The finest painting that ever left the master's easel is that which presents not only a portrait of the little Princess, but also of an interior which tells more of Court life at the time (1656) than pages of written description could do. The tiny Infanta stands in her white satin hooped dress, her hair parted at the side, in the studio of Velazquez, who, with the coveted cross of Santiago upon his breast, is painting a portrait of the King and Queen, whose faces are seen reflected in a mirror at the back of the room, but who do not appear in the picture itself. The child had probably been brought to relieve the tedium of her parents in sitting for their portraits, and seems herself to have grown fretful and needed amusing. The young maid of honour, Donna Maria de Sarmiento, kneels before her, handing her, on a gold salver, a cup of water in the fine red scented clay which it was a vicious fashion of ladies of the day to eat. In the foreground lies a mastiff dozing, and close by it are two of the ugly dwarfs who were such important personages in the Spanish Court, Mari Barbola and Nicolasico Pertusato; whilst behind them, slightly curtseying, is another maid of honour, Dona Isabel de Velasco; and still farther back in the gloom a lady and gentleman in attendance, the former in a conventional dress; whilst in the extreme rear of the picture stands the Queen's quarter-master, Don Jose Nieto, at the open door drawing back a curtain, perhaps that more light may be thrown upon the King and Queen, whom the painter is portraying. The interior of the room, with its special lighting and its unrivalled perspective, fixes for us, as if in a flashlight photograph, one unstudied moment of life in Philip's Court as it was actually passed, and for this reason the picture is invaluable. The existence it crystallizes is a dull one, unrelieved from tedium for Philip except by the presence of his little child, and the trembling consolation of his religion. (Hume, 1927, pp.454–455)

By capturing a moment in the life of the Court, the painting captures its spirit as essentially decadent and overburdened by rules and etiquette. It also conveys the special vulnerability of the child. There is a quality of sadness in her isolation amidst the splendor of her surroundings. The little Princess looks frail in the stiffly ornamental dress, and lonely amidst the excessive attention of her elders. Hume writes of her:

> The favorite child – for Mariana [the Queen] was jealous of the elder, Maria Theresa – was the little Infanta Margaret, born in 1651, a fragile fair little flower of a girl, degenerate from her descent, but not showing excessively the unlovely features she inherited. The etiquette that surrounded the child and her sister was freezing in its formality. Those who served them knelt, and everything had to pass through several hands before reaching them. Their dress, with the wide-hooped farthingales and stiff long bodices, was utterly unchildlike and cumbrous, but, withal, the charm and youth could not be utterly crushed out of Margaret; and Velazquez has left us portraits of her as a child which will always remain the ideal of infancy. (Hume, 1927, pp.453–454)

It was the image of the Princess in the painting which inspired Ravel to write his piano piece *Pavane pour une Infante Défunte* in 1899. He is quoted as instructing a class of music students in Paris:

> Do not attach to the title any more importance than it has. Do not dramatize it. It is not a funeral lament for a dead child but rather an evocation of the pavane which could have been danced by such a little princess as painted by Velazquez at the Spanish Court (Seroff, 1971, p.48).

This is exactly what Jooss choreographed: a pavane that could have been danced by a young princess free in spirit, her innocent, natural childlike qualities contrasting sharply with the stifling atmosphere of the stark and forbidding protocol of the court around her. In his own program notes, Jooss introduced the piece with these words:[10]

> Her spirit imprisoned by the cold and pompous ceremonies of the old Spanish Court, the young Infant seeks in vain to free herself and finally succumbs beneath the burden of its elaborate etiquette.

Jooss's choreography captures the same drama inherent in the painting and in the music. In the painting, this drama is presented through focus and illumination, the contrasting colors and the shading of light and dark. In the music, tension is built by heavy chords that interrupt the airily melancholic theme, all in a gravely measured tempo. In the choreography this drama is expressed by the use of heavy angular movements and a contrasting light circular motion, against a background established by the strict focus of the eyes and the linear traversal of space.

The Pavane as a dance form originated in the sixteenth century courts as a grave and ceremonious dance.[11] The courtiers moved solemnly around in a circle, displaying their finery with proud and haughty carriage. Their pomposity was associated with the strutting of a peacock spreading its tail, displaying its magnificent color and design. The Pavane was in 4/4 time,

danced by couples who performed a simple slow walk, advancing and retreating in a line or a circle (Kirstein, 1969, p.158).
        Synopsis of the ballet.[12]

PAVANE ON THE DEATH OF AN INFANTA

SCENARIO AND CHOREOGRAPHY: Kurt Jooss
MUSIC: *Pavane Pour Une Infante Défunte* (For One Piano), Maurice Ravel
COSTUMES: Sigurd Leeder
PREMIERE: Folkwang Museum, Essen Germany, October, 1929
COMPANY: Folkwang-Tanztheater-Studio
ORIGINAL CAST:
  The Infanta .... Angiola Sartorio
  Ladies of the Court .... Inge Herting, Elsa Kahl, Minni Schniering
  Gentlemen of the Court .. Kurt Jooss, Willy Vogelheim, Ernst Uthoff

DURATION: 5:30 minutes.

SCENARIO

The scene is the Spanish Court; the style is Baroque. Style and place are indicated only through the stylized restrictive costumes and the dramatic lighting. There are no sets. The costumes are constructivistic stylizations of the garments worn in the Spanish Court as it has come down to us through Velazquez's paintings.
        The Gentlemen of the court are dressed in black. They wear tights and short, puffed out or bubbled trousers over them. The "bubbled" quality is indicated by small metal hoops hanging perpendicular to the thigh, like exposed architectural girders, several on each side. The form-fitting vest gives the impression of stiff armor; two large stiff discs encircle the upper arm symbolizing exaggeratedly puffed sleeves. A large, stiff, white double disc serves for a collar, and a short cape hanging from it on the back rounds out the outfit. The tall hats sport an ornament on the left side and the black low-heeled shoes shine with impeccable elegance. The Ladies of the court are in floor length dresses. Their voluminous shiny skirts, made of wine-colored material, stick out aggressively over jagged wire hoops. The material is fine light silk, giving the illusion of weight but enabling the dancers to move easily. Panels of cellophane are sewn into the skirts to make a crinkling sound, exaggerating the illusion of stiffness.[13] Four discs, similar to those of the Gentlemen, adorn their arms from elbow to shoulder. The tight bodice is topped with the same double disc collar. The gray wigs are arranged in corkscrew curls protruding a few inches on either side of the head from under a "V" shaped head ornament.
        The Infanta's dress is simpler, lacking the stiff ornamentation of her elders. She wears light olive green in a pale shade; her skirt is ankle length, leaving her greater freedom of movement. Her white collar is simple; the white cuffs on her sleeves are loosely turned up. Her curls are framed by a large, light, pale pink feather on the right side of her face.
        The lights come up after six measures of the piano music; then the court begins to move. The Ladies and Gentlemen enclose a space whose interior

represents the confines of the court. They move forward and backward in unison in a rigid line, then kneel. The scene is set; they are moving without getting anywhere, without progressing.

The Infanta gently bows to the audience, implicitly greeting the court before her. The kneeling court and this formal courtsey establish at once her rank and knowledge of proper behavior. As she dances she looks timid and shy, but her childish buoyancy is irrepressible and breaks through the veneer of etiquette.

She tries to attract the attention of the courtiers, to dance and play with them, but as she approaches them each in turn rejects her advances. The duty to dance with her falls to the Master of Ceremonies; he takes the Princess' hand with a sweeping gesture. He pauses for a moment with pompous humility before he leads her, keeping a respectful distance, in a short dance. As she goes to him her focus remains on the Gentleman she first approached, beseeching him for human contact. While dancing with the Master of Ceremonies she moves like a marionette as if under his spell. She does as she is told.

She breaks away from him with a small jump, and circles the stage buoyantly. As no one pays attention to her outburst of enthusiasm, she dutifully returns to the Master of Ceremonies and he leads her again in the formal step. As a raw edge appears in the music, the Ladies and Gentlemen advance toward each other to assemble for the pavane, erasing the space in which the Infanta had been dancing. Relentless and impersonal, ignoring her lonely presence, they casually and deliberately crush the Infanta. The physical assault is symbolic of a spiritual destruction. After crossing, the Ladies and Gentlemen join hands, but the gesture is formal: they are caught up in the all-important routine of the court.

The Infanta is left standing alone in their wake. She stops, and as if the will to live has left her she slowly collapses. The gaze of the Ladies focuses on the spot where she would be if she were still standing. Their expressions say: the Princess who was there a moment ago is not there any more. Perhaps she fainted. Perhaps she died.

The choreography

Alan Storey, in an interview entitled *Kurt Jooss on Mime; The Meaning of Steps*, observed that:

> *Pavane* illustrates a tragedy by means of an extremely formal dance pattern; a tragedy enhanced by the complete absence of "mime."
> (Storey, 1943, p.456)

Storey's reference is to the traditional or academic mimetic gestures and expressions that often are superimposed on dance movement. Jooss created dance drama "by using the dancer's body as an inseparable whole and by ensuring that every movement is charged with an expressive value" (Storey 1943, p.456). *Pavane* is a tragedy told entirely by movement. Jooss himself called his dances movement plays: "plays performed by movement instead of words" (Gruen, 1976).

The drama is centered around the vulnerable, lonely figure of the Infanta. She is a royal child free in spirit but confined within the physical and emotional restrictions of the court. She is well versed in the etiquette that governs the life of royalty, but spirited enough to try repeatedly to disregard prescribed behavior in order to establish a more human relationship with those surrounding her. The powerful protocol that rules the behavior of royalty enables the courtiers to ignore the child's wishes even though she ranks above them. As long as they observe the empty formalities and act subservient they do not have to recognize her disturbingly real humanity. The psychological drama lies in the clashing of unequal forces, the power of the court unmatched even by the power of the royal child.

The events and their execution in *Pavane* appear simple, but the motivating forces of the drama are complex and full of subtlety and nuance. This complexity is exhibited in the relationship of the single vulnerable figure of the Infanta to the overbearing unified front of the courtiers. In the course of five minutes we witness an entire spectrum of emotions. The Infanta, vulnerable and trusting, polite but exuberant, turns from a spontaneous, happy child into a bewildered and disappointed waif. The court presents a wall of impenetrability, the uncaring and unchangeable social order. The child-Princess wilts and dies in front of our eyes. Dance critic Deborah Jowitt wrote of the 1976 Joffrey Ballet's production:

> The princess is buoyant; her soft leaps and turns and airy balances curve and circle around their [the courtiers] unyielding lines. Her friendly gestures are answered by frosty bows. When she touches one of the man's hands, she turns for a second into a puppet too. Their interlacing lines seem to stifle her. She wilts to the floor like a plant deprived of light, air, and water. (Jowitt, 1976, p.94)

The message of the ballet must be conveyed through precision in the smallest detail of every movement. For the sake of economy, Jooss deleted one repeated phrase in the musical score (Gruen, 1976).[14] There is no place for frills or decorative embellishment. From the first pavane step in which the courtiers advance in unison, their every movement is a statement, an expressive part of the scenario.

The key dramatic element of the choreography is the contrast between the weighty, linear, rigid movement patterns of the court and the light, free, circular movements of the Infanta. As Jooss himself said:

> Conformity is necessary also between the inner movement of the mind and the outer movement of the body. Again it seems logical that movements of bodily stability should correspond to an inner stability and movements of an unstable nature should be used when the dancer wishes to indicate some psychological vacillation (Storey, 1943, p.454).

The three Gentlemen are lined up in a row, one behind the other, stage right. The five Ladies of the Court stand on a wide diagonal from stage left front to upstage center. The Infanta is alone, center stage, standing with her back to the audience. Her stance suggests her isolation. The courtiers have the right palm stiffly pressed to the heart, the left hand arrogantly placed on the hip. The Ladies cross their elegantly extended hands on top of their panniered skirts. Their posture is stiff, puffed up with pride; their gaze is strictly focused to the front. The two straight lines formed by the Ladies and Gentlemen define the boundaries of the court. Their posture and carriage reflect the court's essence and etiquette.

The pavane step is the cornerstone of the ritual of the court. Jooss has created a modified pavane on six counts: two two-count steps to the sides, then two steps forward. The classic pavane, on twice four or eight counts, advances with the music; the modified step cuts across the music, rejoining it at intervals of twelve counts and twenty-four counts. The power of the movement is reinforced by the dynamics of the step sweeping across the musical measure. This modified pavane step is performed only twice, when the court crosses from side to side and when the Ladies and Gentlemen change places.

This locomotion, both elegant and cumbersome, suggests the prescribed formality of the court and adds psychological weight to its actions. It is a brilliant invention expressing both stubbornness and overriding power. The noble carriage of the courtiers is exaggerated, and they look oppressively pompous. The women hold their arms stiffly forward and out to the sides, elbows out from the shoulders, wrists pointing down, palms turned backwards. The upper torso is bent slightly forward. This posture gives the Ladies the look of a puffed up turkey. The men, with their hands on heart and hip, portray arrogance and superiority. Their kneeling pose in front of the Princess reflects no genuine humility, only cold impersonal etiquette.

Movement and pose are both highly stylized. The gentlemen take two large legato steps forward and kneel down, their bodies assuming an angular form. The ladies perform a low reverence to the floor. Their backs are straight, the arms are held to the sides, the elbows bent, the wrists straight, fingers pointing downward. The two rows are facing each other; each pose is a frieze.

At all times the Infanta's movements are confined within the court defined by the two lines of courtiers, an invincible front. Her first bow is a small stiff curtsey, and after a few steps forward she begins to dance. Her steps are light and her arms move freely as she approaches the Gentleman upstage, then the Lady in front, then the Gentleman in front. The latter bows with ceremonial reverence and then resumes his aloof pose. Then the Gentleman in the middle serving as a Master of Ceremonies moves to the center with two large strides. He takes the Infanta by the hand and leads her in a circular path. She obediently accompanies him with a broken-winged mechanical movement. Her arms are held upright, echoing the posture of the Ladies; her torso bends to the left and she bows mechanically as she takes the final few steps. The master of ceremonies looks away from her as he leads her; she looks like a small broken puppet.

The movements of the Ladies and Gentlemen of the court are measured and weighty, earthbound and powerful. In contrast, the Infanta moves in airy circular patterns. When she approaches the courtiers, asking them to dance with her, her movements are spontaneous and her gestures friendly. Then she runs downstage and lunges on the diagonal, her gaze focused beyond the court, her arms reaching out beseechingly. She looks to the outside world, yearning for freedom. Meanwhile the court has formed a semicircle behind her. The Ladies and Gentlemen are changing places; each line crosses over to the other side of the stage in a large semicircle. They step stiffly with the artificial formality of the pavane. When they reach their places they kneel down in reverence once again.

The Princess hops lightly, her feet flicker in the air, her body bends like a willow and she lands softly like a fallen leaf. The court has risen, and suddenly the Ladies and Gentlemen take a firm step toward her. The two lines converge on her from opposite directions. The Infanta, alarmed, rises on tiptoe, and begins to move from side to side with rapid small steps center stage. Her hands are clasped together in front of her, the shoulders slightly raised in a gesture of helplessness. The two lines of the court meet and pass through each other as the Infanta moves between them with small gliding bourrées, glancing fearfully from side to side as their advance crushes her in their midst. The court turns sharply to the back of the stage after completing the crossing. The Ladies and Gentlemen turn toward one another and take partners to begin the pavane. When they join hands, fingertips touching, the gesture is purely formal and impersonal. They finish exactly as they began.

The Infanta ducks out from beneath the extended arms of the last couple, turns around and stiffly and tentatively follows the court. She takes two side steps and a few broken bourrées. The court separates at the rear of the stage, turning and striding back to the original position, heads snapping sharply from left to right. The Princess teeters, slowly weakens, then sinks to the floor. Her left arm rises upward in a small signal, a last gesture of helplessness, then it too drops to the side in complete defeat.

The statement and the message

As exemplified in *Pavane*, society has banded together against the individual. The community is unwilling to accept behavior that threatens the established order. Nonconformity, even that of a royal child, is suppressed. Marcia Siegel observes:

> The princess is vulnerable, overwhelmed by the formidable and cold process of royal behavior. Jooss is saying that the monarch is as victimized as her subjects. (Siegel, 1977, p.149)

The representatives of the old rigid social order reject the spontaneity of the young. Unable and unwilling to respond, society destroys what it does not understand and therefore finds threatening. The ballet is a statement about the specific rigidities of court life, and about the ever-threatened value of freedom in opposition to the implacable forces that blindly oppose it.

On a more universal level, Jooss wants to show in this ballet the beauty and fragility of the free human spirit. What better way to show this than through the figure of a vulnerable child. The Infanta stands not only for personal freedom but also for that intangible inner quality we value so much. It is associated with spontaneous expression, experimentation, curiosity and artistic creativity. If this human quality is not nurtured it withers away and dies, like the little Princess of *Pavane*.

The Dance of Death

Death is inescapable. It makes no exceptions: rich or poor, genius or simpleton, death takes us all. This idea of death as the great equalizer was the main theme of a bizarre medieval ritual called the Dance of Death. Neither king or peasant could escape this final act, and to the satisfaction of the poor and powerless, all distinctions of status and riches disappeared. To this consoling idea, a moral concept was later added: each person's death is a result of his way of life. Since death is the final act in a series of actions that reflect a person's character, each person is responsible in a way for the manner of his death.

The Dance of Death originated from a combination of fertility rites, sympathetic magic and miracle-plays. The ancient mystery cults of death and resurrection ensured the fertility of the land and conferred immortality on culture heroes. These sources became incorporated into Christianity and Church ritual to form the Dance of Death, or Dance Macabre. It consisted of a fantastic processional through churchyards and cemeteries, led by the figure of Death as a hooded skeleton.

This grotesque ceremony reflected the desperate social and economic conditions of feudalism and the recurrent devastation of the plague. To the poor it was some consolation that wealth and rank did not give protection against the epidemic; for the Church it was an allegory of the frivolity of human vanity. It was a rehearsal for the Last Judgment where no one can hide from the final verdict. In the midst of devastation, this ritual occasionally took on an aura of defiantly mad gaiety.

Our knowledge of the Dance of Death comes from literature and art. The first representations of it are wall paintings in churches. The earliest are in a medieval church in Klingenthal, Switzerland and in the Church of the Holy Innocents in Paris. There are well-known frescos in churches in Dresden, Lucerne and London, and friezes in Tallinn and in the famous Marienkirche in Lübeck. The idea of choreographing a dance of death first came to Jooss when he saw the frieze in the Marienkirche. Sadly, this frieze was destroyed in the Second World War. In the Lübecker *Totentanz* Death was a skeletal figure wrapped in a white cloth, holding hands and dancing with people from all walks of life.

Among the most striking later depictions are the woodcuts of the Dance of Death by Hans Holbein. Holbein's Death is a quick-footed and agile skeleton. He twists, turns, beats on a tambourine or fights with bone and shield as he takes the Lady, the Nun, the Soldier, the Bishop, and the King and Queen. Holbein's woodcuts are distinctive for the individuality of each victim. Although they are representative of a class or a profession, each of them expresses personal pain, horror, and grief. Death tirelessly maneuvers each individual into the inevitable final duet. The drama is similar in Jooss's ballet, *The Green Table*, where Death steps forth at the appropriate moment to claim each victim.

The inspiration for a ballet has rarely been documented as thoroughly as in the case of *The Green Table*. Jooss told the story of its creation in numerous interviews.[15] The entire process, from the planting of the first seed in Jooss's imagination to his presentation of the ballet in Paris, took ten years. Of course, he did not work steadily on the ballet; it was a process of repeatedly toying with the idea of a Dance of Death. Toward the end, when the perfect opportunity arose, he very nearly decided not to choreograph the piece at all.

The process began when he was working with the *Tanzbühne Laban* in Gleschendorf during the summer of 1922. While visiting the nearby city of Lübeck, he was deeply moved by the famous fresco in the *Marienkirche*. In an oral history interview he describes his first impression:

> I'd seen the famous Lübecker Totentanz, a sequence of pictures of all sorts of people dancing with Death who was portrayed as a skeleton. It seems to have been in the medieval period when people's minds were occupied with this kind of dancing, which actually was a symbolic expression for the fact that everyone would die the way he had lived. Death danced with the beggar with the bagpipe, and it was quite nice, an obviously jolly dance. In another picture he danced with a middle-aged peasant woman who had a baby in her arms, obviously dead born, a still-born baby. Probably she also died with this childbirth, and that dance was very gentle in the movement one could see. (Tobias, 1976, pp. 2; 6)

Two years later, he saw a group of actors perform a *Totentanz* whose motif was taken from those same Lübecker wall paintings. Again the theme impressed him.

In 1926, while on tour with Leeder, Jooss made his first attempt at creating a Dance of Death. His plan was to dance Death first with a scythe; then he and Leeder would alternate, wearing a series of masks, each representing a different character dancing a duet with an invisible Death. Leeder completed eight masks for the project but the dance was never choreographed because of Jooss's incapacitating knee injury.[16]

Another source of movement ideas was a character that Jooss created for the 1930 production of Georg Keiser's play *Europa* at the *Düsseldorfer Schauspielhaus*. Keiser was one of the most inventive Expressionist playwrights of the time. The director's idea was to use slides to portray the metamorphosis in which Zeus turns into an angry bull. Jooss was invited as a guest artist for the role of Zeus, and he volunteered to dance the transformation scene instead of using slides. He did it with great success. F. A. Cohen composed and conducted the music for the production. Jooss remembers:

> That was in 1930. Anyway, my friend Fritz Cohen, my wife and I worked every evening on that bull. Once on the way home I said to Aino (Siimola): "I must make a ballet where I can be such a beast, it's wonderful. I would like to work on the idea." I forgot about it, but in the end the bull became the way to the figure of Death in *The Green Table*. Together with that I also had the Gentlemen in Black around this table. That had come as counteraction to the bull which, later on, transferred itself into *The Green Table*. (Huxley, 1982, p.8)

The Green Table is more than just a Dance of Death; it integrates that theme with the idea of the all-destructive force of war. War is an arena

in which Death becomes the ultimate victor. This second idea was inspired
by the terrible experiences of World War I and the ominous shadow that
National Socialism was casting on Germany by the early 1930's. Jooss had
become alarmed at the danger of another war from his avid reading of Carl
von Ossietsky's leftist periodical *Die Weltbühne*. The main contributor was
Kurt Tucholsky; he was exposing the German military's secret rearmament
and warning of preparations for a new war.

At the end of 1931, Jooss was asked to enter the choreographic
competition at *Les Archives Internationales de la Danse* in Paris. Jooss's
initial conception for the ballet was centered upon an evil figure, the god
Mammon, emerging from a box-like table around which the Gentlemen in
Black, as bankers, play out their drama. Their feuding releases this evil
destructive force (Huxley, 1982, p.9). Jooss changed this entire concept during
the six weeks it took him to complete the work. In *The Green Table* it has
become Death who is unleashed by the Gentlemen in Black to preside
triumphantly over the war events which are the consequence of their actions.
In an interview with Walter Terry, Jooss spoke with wonder of his cooperation
with composer F. A. Cohen during those six weeks: "He improvised like
magic. We worked like one person on it; we could never account for it"
(Terry, 1967).

As the *Folkwang Tanzbühne* was en route to Paris for the competition,
Jooss remembers saying "I feel very clearly, this piece will be a tremendous
success or an unheard-of theatrical scandal" (Huxley, 1982, p.10). The
competition was held from the second to the fourth of July, 1932. Jooss's
ballet was eleventh on the program of twenty works, the fourth out of six
pieces performed on July third. The announcement in French read:

> La troupe FOLKWANGTANZBÜHNE DE LA VILLE D'ESSEN
> (Allem.) "LA TABLE VERTE" Danse macabre de Kurt Jooss.
> Musique de F. A. Cohen. Choreographie de Kurt Jooss. Costumes
> de Hein Heckroth.

The work was an instant success. In later years Jooss recalled that the response
of the audience was incredible.

> They nearly clapped through the whole piece, which was dreadful,
> but of course we liked it because it showed us that we had
> succeeded. (Huxley, 1982, p.10)

When asked about Laban's reaction, Jooss added: "He was one of the judges.
He cried. He was overjoyed" (Huxley, 1982, p.10).

Immediately after the competition Jooss went on tour with the ballet.
He counted close to 4000 performances before he stopped counting (Terry,
1967). Since its creation *The Green Table* has never been out of repertory.
The United States premiere was in New York City on October 31, 1933,
at the Forrest Theater. The performers were the Ballets Jooss, with Kurt
Jooss himself as Death. People who saw him in the role remember it as
an extraordinry performance. In 1967 the Joffrey Ballet became the first
American company to produce *The Green Table*.

Synopsis of the ballet.

THE GREEN TABLE

BOOK AND CHOREOGRAPHY: Kurt Jooss
MUSIC: F. A. Cohen (for two pianos)
COSTUMES: Hein Heckroth
PREMIERE: July 3, 1932
ORIGINAL CAST:

Death	Kurt Jooss
The Standard Bearer	Ernst Uthoff
The Young Soldier	Walter Wurg
The Old Soldier	Rudolf Pescht
The Young Girl	Lisa Czobel
The Woman	Elsa Kahl
The Old Mother	Frida Holst
The Profiteer	Karl Bergeest

The Gentlemen in Black, The Soldiers,
   The Women: Lola Botka, Frida Holst, Elsa Kahl, Lucie
Lenzner, Masha Lidolt, Hertha Lorenz, Trude
Pohl, Karl Bergeest, Rudolf Pescht, Heinz Rosen,
Ernst Uthoff, Peter Wolff, Walter Wurg, Hans
Züllig

ORDER OF SCENES:
1. The Gentlemen in Black
2. The Farewells
3. The Battle
4. The Refugees
5. The Partisan
6. The Brothel
7. The Aftermath
8. The Gentlemen in Black

DURATION: 35 minutes.

SCENARIO

The Gentlemen in Black (Prologue). The curtain rises following a few powerful, ominous, measured chords of musical introduction. The music softens to a sarcastically pleasant little tango. On the two sides of a long rectangular green table are positioned ten elderly gentlemen. The table looks like a felt-top conference table. It is foreshortened and slopes upward toward the back: the audience perceives it as flat, yet its whole surface is visible. The men are in tuxedos and white gloves. Each wears a mask with exaggerated features. With one exception they are exceedingly bald with longish fringes of gray, red or dark scraggly hair. Their foreheads are high and bumpy, their expressions are supercilious. Some have drooping mustaches and one

has a long gray beard. They are obvious caricatures but they take themselves
with deadly seriousness. They are the power brokers, and they are in deep
disagreement. Each side of the table represents a faction.

At first their debate preserves the veneer of civilized behavior. There
is no discernible right or wrong side; the opposing forces are exactly equal
in number and demeanor. They spy on each other's conversation, or pretend
to be disinterested. Slowly shedding the mannerisms of upbringing, they lose
their temper and begin to slap the table. Insincerity oozes from every gesture.
The essence of this conference is that nobody means what he says and nobody
says what he means.

Realizing at last that agreement is out of the question, they line up at
the front of the stage. As if on command each draws a small revolver from
his breast pocket. For a moment the two factions threaten each other with
revolvers aimed. But then, in ultimate solidarity with their kind, they face
the audience and simultaneously discharge their revolvers into the air. The
stage goes dark. War has been declared, but others will do the fighting.

Invisible in the dark, men and table vanish as a rumbling rolling piano
chord is played. Then, in front of the black curtains which frame the entire
stage area, the figure of Death becomes visible. He is a combination of soldier
and skeleton. Black leather straps outline his rib cage and pad his shoulders
like protruding joints. The bones of his legs and arms show black on his
light gray colored costume. A black leather shield on his hips is a skeletal
reminder of pelvic bone. His face is skull-like, eyes black sockets, nose and
cheeks hollow. On his head a military helmet is made taller by a large comb.
Loose-topped midcalf boots echo the shape of comb and pelvic shield. He
is large, self-assured and arrogant. A gladiator in the guise of a skeleton,
he plunges brutally into a powerful solo.

Death here is an incarnation who knows his time has come, his time
to rule as a warrior. He moves to an insistent beat which is a musical evocation
of the underworld. Death has been conjured up and given free rein. He
proudly pulls himself up to his full height. Briefly extending his arms to
the sides, he takes the position of a cross projecting his power to the four
corners of the world. Insistently but methodically he begins to mobilize his
forces. He beats an endless time with his feet as he raises and lowers his
fists. The flow of time itself is an act of his will and a manifestation of
his invincible power.

The Farewells. To the insistent timeless beat of Death, the troops sign
up for battle. First to arrive is the Standard Bearer. He gestures forcefully
with a white flag that cleaves the air with sharp snapping reports. His uniform
consists of a silver helmet, gray tights and a white harness across his chest:
a stylized version of a uniform from the Great War. He marches proudly
and the music takes on heroic tones. He is joined by three soldiers in similar
outfits, eager, enthusiastic, moving vigorously, training with imaginary
bayonets and swearing alliance to the glorious flag.

Next comes a soldier followed by The Young Girl. She does not want
him to go, but he joins the other soldiers on the march as she slowly pulls
away. Meanwhile a trio, the Old Soldier, his Old Mother and a woman arrive.
Again the farewells are painful, but duty calls and he joins his comrades
as the woman and the mother comfort each other. The two younger women
wear plain mid-calf length dresses with short sleeves, one in pale yellow and

the other in flaming red. The Mother wears a full-length brown dress with long sleeves covering her arms and a scarf-like gray bonnet tied under her chin. The younger ones' heads are wrapped in tightly rolled head scarves.

Suddenly the Profiteer enters. He is dressed in black tights and white tee-shirt, white gloves on his hands and white spats. With bowler hat in hand he salutes the crowd. As the soldiers begin to move he starts clapping, urging on the procession. As they march into battle with imaginary bayonets drawn, Death looms large in front of them. He stands with outstretched arms, under which the soldiers pass on their way to battle. The woman in red, after a moment's doubt, resolutely joins them. She becomes The Partisan Woman, thereby deciding her fate. Meanwhile the Profiteer notices the prostrate figure of the Young Girl, and swoops down upon her like a bird of prey. With a slight turn of his torso, Death acknowledges his first victory. Everyone on stage has passed into his realm.

The Battle. On the battlefield the fight rages around the flag. It has lost its pristine whiteness and bears traces of blood and mud. In hand-to-hand combat bodies are punched, shoved, beaten, and slashed with imaginary weapons. The flag, a sacred symbol for which blood flows, is always in sight. The two sides, equal, dressed alike and looking alike, attempt to keep or to take possession of the flag. In orderly and repetitious battle, the participants group and re-group. It is a brutal but predictable scene: formations engage in combat, the dying fall, and the living urge each other on.

Suddenly, unexpectedly, as if emerging from a whirlwind, Death appears, rising to his full height in center stage. In his left fist he grips the wrist of a dying soldier. He lets go contemptuously, without looking, an easy victory, and the soldier falls to the ground. The battle field is strewn with corpses. Death begins his first victory march. High-stepping and pompous, he is a dark knight, detached and powerful, leaving a well-accomplished work on the battle field.

He has hardly exited when agitated chords signal the arrival of the Profiteer. Cat-like, he wends his way among the corpses looking for opportunity. With delight he spots a ring, probably a gold wedding band. He slips it from the dead finger and examines it, turning it this way and that. Perhaps sensing that he has strayed too close to the wake of Death, he leaps over the corpse he has just plundered and rushes off.

The Refugees. A slow sad ballad accompanies a slow-moving group of women led by the Old Mother and including the Young Girl. Fearful, hugging, helping each other, they travel on strange terrain. Surveying the unknown, the Old Mother is afraid, but resigned; to her it doesn't matter any more. Moving to a voice that only she can hear, she is caught in an ever-narrowing circle. The music luring her on has a sweet tone; it is almost a lullaby. Then a harsh chord is struck and the light shows Death, crouched in wait, beginning to rise. The refugee women freeze in their tracks and stare at the rising figure with horror. The Old Mother is supported by the Young Girl as the others run. Death lifts his arms invitingly but with clenched fists that regally affirm his will.

Slumped in the arms of The Young Girl, the Old Mother listens to Death calling. She makes a feeble attempt to flee, but Death extends his arms in an invitation. The Mother moves in a trance toward Death. He takes her outstretched hand and leads here in a courtly dance. Then suddenly he points out the unmistakable way to the end. When she is resigned to go he picks her up, gently cradling her like a child in his arms, and carries her out impassively.

Once again the Profiteer appears as Death leaves. This time it is the Young Girl, prostrate with grief, who attracts his attention. Lacking the strength to escape him, she lets herself be led away.

The Partisan. Eloquently heroic and uplifting chords herald the arrival of the Partisan Woman. Holding a long pale yellow scarf in outstretched arms above her head, she leaps high off the ground in long strides, circles around and signals with the scarf like a semaphore. She whips it from side to side, a symbol of liberation and of the homemade, makeshift weaponry of guerrillas and revolutionaries everywhere. Tucking her weapon into her belt, she undertakes her brave but hopeless mission. Though committed and passionate, she must still conquer her moments of doubt and fear. She gathers her strength, rising to ever greater heights of fervor and self-sacrifice.

Scouting the area, she lies low on the ground as the first line of troops arrives. These are not the vigorous enthusiastic soldiers we saw in battle. They are battle-weary heavy-footed troops on a long march. The Partisan reconnoiters, her resolve building. As the second line of soldiers moves by she pursues them, catching up to the last soldier in the line and flicking her scarf around his neck. As he falls to the ground, Death steps out behind him, arms out in the powerful position of the cross. Simultaneously three soldiers appear and train their guns on The Partisan. Death folds his arms and begins to move toward her. She sees the soldiers and Death approaching; an invisible string pulls her to the execution ground. With great deliberation Death steps behind her, lifts his arms, and in a staccato movement signals the firing squad to kill.

The Brothel. Prostitutes and soldiers sway in hurried sensuality to a jazzy waltz. The Young Girl, procured by the Profiteer, stands alone, frightened. The Profiteer shows her off to his customers; he claps his hands and forces her to pay attention. Fearfully and reluctantly, she accepts the first soldier, who grabs her and rushes her through a brutal duet. The next soldier approaches savagely and pulls her into another merciless duet. A third follows; she crumples to the floor. The Profiteer signals the company to leave and offers the Young Girl to the last waiting soldier. He pulls her up and they engage in a semi-tender duet, his lust tempered by her battered fragility and his need for momentary human companionship. In this instant of vulnerability Death steps in to take the place of her last lover. He pulls her into a final sadistic high-stepping dance, driving her mercilessly until she willingly steps into his arms seeking rest. He bends over her in a final carnal embrace, then stares at the audience, insatiable.

The Aftermath. Death, crouched behind the Old Soldier and shadowing his movements, takes the flag from him effortlessly and the two of them begin the processional. All of the dead join in, forming a long row: the Old Soldier still gripping Death's arm, the Partisan Woman, the Old Mother, a soldier, the Young Girl, more soldiers. They march in a circle, frozen in the postures characteristic of their manner of death. Death in the middle is holding up the flag tainted with blood and dirt; they all march to his rhythm now. At Death's command the dead slump to the floor and lie still. At this moment the Standard Bearer bursts upon the stage in a replay of his first entrance. His inspirited music and enthusiasm are quickly withered by the stare of Death, and he joins the ghastly procession as it leaves the scene.

Now the Profiteer enters on his last prowl. He senses danger and looks searchingly for its source. Suddenly he finds himself face to face with Death. Death advances in large powerful strides and the Profiteer backs away, trying to escape. But it is too late; he is already caught in Death's sphere, no matter how he twists, turns and scurries about. Death ignores the Profiteer: a minor irritant, a cockroach on its last run. While preparing for his final victory solo, Death sweeps up the wriggling Profiteer.

All have died. Death, his task accomplished, dances to celebrate his power. The war has given him a wonderful feast, but he remains implacable, insatiable, ever ready for his awesome task. With an unexpected movement he vanishes from the stage as swiftly as he had appeared.

The Gentlemen in Black (Epilogue). The lighting comes up to reveal the Gentlemen in Black standing in a row, exactly as we had left them. We hear again the shot fired simultaneously from their pistols. Tucking the pistols back into their breast pockets, they file back to the table and take up the exact positions they held at the beginning. Again the argument takes place in exactly the same gestures, with one difference: this time their movements create no sound. When they bang on the table we cannot hear it: the fake drama is now even further from reality. Visually the action and the world are the same, but the experience of Death has distanced us so that we now see it *sub specie aeternitatis*.

The dramatic themes

The Green Table has two main themes: its treatment of death and its anti-war message. To anthropomorphize, to give human qualities to the forces of nature, is a characteristic of human thinking. When death is given a human form, even if it be a skeleton, this is an attempt to understand the essentially incomprehensible, our own mortality. The personification of Death is the most significant element of *The Green Table*. Awesome in appearance, a combination of heraldic knight, soldier and skeleton, Death provides the connecting thread of the story.

With the pistol shot of the prologue, Death has received a special mandate. Since war is now declared, he appears as a soldier. The job which he ordinarily does quietly and discreetly in bedrooms and hospital rooms can now be done publicly with fanfare. Man has played into his hand, making his job easy. He has no need to find and stalk his prey: it comes to him of its own accord. His appearance brings a chill into the air. He is bathed in a greenish light, his skeletal features immobile. With him comes a temporary suspension of the ordinary rules of existence. The duration of war is an extraordinary time, a time of natural disaster. Once let loose, war is like a great storm; it gathers momentum, sweeps everything before it, and subsides only after spending its fury.

Since War lets the forces of destruction loose, the ideas of War and Death are inextricably intertwined. War is the arena in which Death performs. The forces of evil lie not in Death itself, but in the powers at the conference table who let Death reap an untimely and rich harvest. Death himself is fearsome but impartial; he only collects what is duly his. Each person's fate has been decided and the mode of his death is a consequence of his own way of life. Death adapts himself to every circumstance.

Death has no disguise but many faces. They appear in his manner of treating each of his victims. He is cold, hard and merciless with the armies who massacre each other, making his task absurdly easy. As a superior warrior he steps into their midst and suddenly the battlefield is strewn with corpses. He is firm but courtly toward the Old Mother, compelling in his call but gentle in his approach. As captain of the firing squad, he invokes the fate that the Partisan Woman dared to face. He is rough but sensuous with the Young Girl, and she finds peace in his final lover's embrace. He is impatient with the Profiteer, heedlessly caught up in the same web he used to ensnare his victims. Death does not have to fight for the lives of these people. Each character is doomed, and as Death wills them to die, their will merges with his.

Dramatically each character is larger than life, representative not only of a type but of a whole class of people. Critic Allen Storey wrote that in Jooss's ballets

> figures become units, soldiers become armies, brothels turn into nations where mental prostitution is rife and intelligence is dulled with craving for pleasure. (Storey, 1940, p.596)

The Old Mother represents all mothers who suffer loss in war, and the worn-out elders who have come to the end of their road and accept the call of death. The Young Girl is all women brutalized by men, for whom death offers welcome relief. The soldiers represent the youthful conscripts of all nations, mobilized with visions of glory and ending up dead on the battlefield, their ideals as soiled as their flags. The Profiteer stands for all those who take advantage of other people's misery and think they can get away with it: those who fish in muddy waters and welcome the disasters they cleverly turn to their advantage. The Gentlemen in Black represent the special interests of power, greed, prejudice, intolerance and the various ideologies, all those petty prides and jealousies which turn nation against nation and cause the suffering and devastation of war. The dramatic format of the ballet, A B C B A (where A is the Gentlemen in Black, and B is the defining solo by Death), gives a cyclical character to the ballet. When Death suddenly disappears after his final solo, we know that he remains nearby, waiting for man to give him his next opportunity to seize the helm of history.

The choreography

The opening scene paints a wicked caricature of the power brokers. Self-important, supercilious and calculating, each character casts a comic but frightening figure. From the first moment, a constant communication is occurring around the table. They are real human beings, not puppets as is often stated. They are anonymous but their masks are designed to exaggerate individual characteristics. They are engaged in a conversation of global importance. Their decisions will affect the lives of millions, yet they remain devious and deceitful. They show off the imaginary medals on their chests, and engage in heated arguments. They throw up their hands in dismay, insist on a point with raised finger, nod or shake their heads, listening, lecturing or clapping. Gesture is the essence of the choreography here; through the stylized gesturing we understand the motivation of these characters.

Five Gentlemen are "sitting" at each side of the table. Actually they are squatting in a pose that simulates sitting. The tableau comes alive as each figure turns to face his neighbor with his arms raised: questioning and explaining, incredulous and argumentative. As they turn back, the last Gentleman on the right stands up and shakes his raised arms, palms open, in an impatient gesture: "Gentlemen, don't you understand?!" This gesture occurs several times and it always stands out clearly, a warning and an admonition. The "philosopher", an old man with a long white beard, repeatedly poses with a pointed finger: an important idea! He is pompous, self-important and sarcastic as he claps mockingly at intervals.

The "dreamer" is right front: his elbow rests on the table and he stares into space. An accusing finger is thrust toward him from the opposite side. When this opponent is moved to action he puts an outstretched leg insolently on the table, or jumps on top of it and shakes his fists. They all periodically slap the table with open palms. A Gentleman on the left cups a hand to his ear trying to overhear his opponents' private conversations. In a highly ingenious movement they all lean horizontally over the table and with lowered foreheads push toward each other. This gesture feigns deference with a bow, while suggesting an aggressive bull-like readiness to lock horns. Straightening, they tilt backward proudly or sway back and forth. Sometimes one side tilts forward while the other tilts backward like a see-saw. These variations are quite comical, but they build an increasingly agitated mood around the table. At one point, using the table for support, they all push off, piercing the air in back with their legs.

As the argument gets heated they march away from the table, hands clasped in fists. They lobby in small groups, each facing an opponent. They slice the air with chopping gestures, count on their fingers, or shake their palms in a gesture of "No!" Finding no agreement, they walk around agitated, torso bent parallel to the ground as if wisdom or solutions could be found there. Frustrated and furious, they take up fencing positions, thrust and parry. Quickly realizing the folly of this action, they bow to their opponent. Then with a mechanically bouncing little toe-heel step, one hand tucked into the lapel and the other swinging by the side, all return to their original positions at the table.

Having failed to reach an agreement they begin to move in unison with military precision and purpose. The factions form up in separate lines at the front of the stage. Swiftly and elegantly they pluck small revolvers from their breast pockets. Facing each other they crouch and aim for a moment. In an instant they realize the possible consequences, bow low with the sweep of an arm, face outward, and fire into the air. Let others do their dirty work.

The covert aggression and overt politeness of the Gentlemen in Black keeps the tension at a high level. Their gestures exhibit their calculating and deceptive nature; they pontificate, threaten, swagger and spy. They are inflexible but agile in jockeying for advantage. The tone echoes the gravity of the situation. Its mood turns more severe as tempers rise. The last chords turn into a menacing drum roll that foreshadows the arrival of Death.

There is a stunning contrast between the comic figures and facile gestures of the Gentlemen in Black and the stark appearance and commanding motions of Death. We are plunged from light to darkness, from a realm of playful if sinister sophistication to one of brutal and deadly realities.

Death rises from a wide deep knee bend, shifting his weight and straddling space, pulling himself up from the underworld, his arms gathering strength from the earth. As he reaches his full height he begins to move, his arms wielding his characteristic trademark, the scythe. Leaning slightly and shifting his weight, he raises this imaginary scythe and brings it down with closed fists. He cuts through space, slashing the air on a plane in front of himself with open palms. All the while his feet are stomping in a steady six-beat pulse. Concentrated in this sweeping rhythmic movement is a devastating show of power and purpose.

Death moves proudly as he cocks his head, tilts backward like a rearing horse, and thrusts a knee out in front. At the same time he raises one clenched fist above his head, holding the other in front of his body. He has risen on the ball of one foot and for a second he holds this pose, his outline etched in space. Then with a quick change of direction he pierces the air with a swift backward kick and slices the space above it with a horizontal chop of the hand. With arms raised he grabs at the sky on both sides of his body. Bringing them down he gathers in the space in front of him. The world belongs to him and there are no limits to his power. He leaps into the air with a turn; landing on the diagonal he thrusts with his arms as if wielding a sword. Then with one arm sweeping above his head he again projects his power over space, as if encircling it with a rope or capturing it in a net.

In this forceful solo, using only a few precisely crafted movement combinations, Death conjures up the images of horseman, coachman, swordsman and grim reaper: all the imagery associated with death from the Middle Ages. His steady, rhythmic stomp marks the passage of time, his greatest weapon. The scope of his power is made palpable by the dynamics of his movement and its mastery of the surrounding space. The solo is accompanied by an eerie, insistent drum roll on the pianos and the heavy staccato echoes of his stomping feet.

Our first image of Death is as a brutal destructive force. But Death proves to be as versatile as the diverse ways of dying; he presents a new face in each situation. He calls the armies to war, endowing them with his own physical power. Marching in place, he rhythmically flexes and relaxes his biceps, ratcheting his forearms up and down. The ingenious combination of four steps in place achieves the double effect of a marching soldier and a figure eternally marking time.

In each episode Death appears suddenly, always at the climax, the moment when his time and consequently his victim's time has come. At the end of the battle scene he rises up out of a whirlwind of fighting and dying soldiers. He stands tall and strong among the wounded, his arms extended to the sides, fists clenched. He surveys the scene like a general on his high-stepping horse, pulling in his reins. He is both horse and horseman in this brutally elegant movement.

With the Old Mother he plays the Knight. He turns to her in a compelling calling gesture, one arm held high and one extended toward her, palms invitingly opened, three fingers extended in unholy benediction. He ritualistically holds two extended fingers up as in a church ceremony. He lowers himself to one knee in front of her and she bows to him in reverence. Stepping behind her with a cavalier bounce in his step, hands on his right hip where the hilt of a sword would be, he leads her in a few measured steps and she follows graciously. Then like a semaphore he tilts, pointing out her path with a compelling motion of his hand. She turns away once in horror, then gives in to his will and settles herself in his arms. Unrelenting but knightly, he slowly walks away cradling the Old Mother's dead body.

With The Partisan Woman, Death is as relentless as the fate which she chose when she decided to kill. His arms hug his own body and then lift upward in front as if he is folding himself in an imaginary cape. Then he turns to stand behind her as the soldiers line up to form the firing squad. She opens her arms wide; Death raises his folded arms above his head. As she is shot he opens his arms into the cross position as she slowly turns and falls at his feet. Death places two hands on a hip and lifts his head in triumph.

He is most expansive with the Young Girl, relishing the role of seducer. As her final human partner approaches her, Death appears dogging his steps. The man steps blindly past her − having slipped into the realm of death, she is invisible to him − and it is Death who takes her outstretched hands. With large powerful strides Death begins his seduction as brutally as the soldiers in the brothel. He grabs her by the buttocks and pulls her tightly to him. After a few steps in this vulgar embrace he takes her hand and sweeps her around him in a large circle. His right arm is swinging above his head as if wielding a whip, and he skips in place, literally driving the Young Girl to her destruction. After this pitiless recapitulation of her humiliation Death wraps her in a tender final embrace, offering solace as her savior. He rocks her gently to the floor and bends low over her prone figure, sensuous and victorious in his double conquest.

From the Old Soldier Death seizes the flag which he believed in and fought for. Rising up behind him, Death grabs the flag and takes possession of the Old Soldier's life. In the presence of Death, the Standard Bearer's exaltation fades away with his life, and he becomes just one more puppet-like corpse in the final procession.

The last to die is the Profiteer. He jumps on stage with outstretched arms at the very moment when Death arrives to perform his final victory dance. The Profiteer is the opposite of Death in every way. While Death stands tall, erect and imposing, the Profiteer bends low and crouches furtively. His body is coiled and curved; he springs like a cat and slithers like a snake. While Death moves in a heavy staccato and angular manner, the Profiteer hops and skips, moving as if through a medium lighter than that which ordinary mortals occupy. He is a mercurial wheeler-dealer, a sociopath, thief, pimp and coward.

In the brothel he pushes and shoves the Young Girl into the embrace of the lecherous soldiers. Playing the host, he claps for attention as he manipulates his women into the arms of his clientele; then he rubs his hands together in delight. Spreading his palms, he shows off his merchandise like a satisfied businessman. As he leaves the Young Girl alone with the soldier who bought her he exits backward, scraping and bowing in deference to the only power he knows: profit. Faced with death, the Profiteer uses all his ingenuity in an attempt to escape. He traverses the stage with a remarkable series of forward and backward steps, curious and fearful, shielding his eyes as he peers about. When he sees Death approaching he shrinks back in horror. He ducks down into a crouch and tries to elude him by shifting directions. Death pays no attention to him and plunges into a repetition of his opening solo. What was then a recruiting march is now a victory dance. As it becomes more heated and savage the Profiteer lunges and runs desperately. Death holds him on an invisible string. The Profiteer hurls himself to the floor repeatedly, his legs shoot upward as his face is pressed into the ground. Death sweeps him up without missing a beat. The Profiteer rolls out in a somersault like a clump of weed carried off by the wind.

The world in which Death collects his dues is defined by War; everyone is a war victim. The women have lost sons, husbands or lovers, and many become refugees. The Old Mother leads the refugee women, walking before them with small steps, fearful but resigned for she has little left to lose. She is supported by the Young Girl who would have been her daughter-in-law in time of peace. Her body is bent and frail, one arm hanging from a crooked elbow like the broken wing of a bird. She clasps her hands in prayer, then peers ahead shielding her eyes. Looking into the future and afraid of what she has seen, she shrinks back and finds refuge in memory. With rocking steps she pats the air with her hands, like the top of a remembered child's head. Her arms move in soft large circles; then as reality intrudes she claws at the air and runs in concentric circles like an animal in a cage. When Death beckons she lifts a hand to her ear: she hears his call and knows it is meant for her. Supported in a deep knee bend, her body sagging in complete resignation, she lifts an arm and begins her slow approach to him.

The Partisan is all courage and determination. She shoots across space in a straight line, her hands holding a scarf stretched tight above her head. She turns, signals, coils her body tightly and drops low to the ground, ready to attack. Her movements alternate between a tightly stretched line, ready to snap with tension, and a spiraling curve that coils and uncoils, gathering strength and fury. Searching for the enemy, her upward jumps and low crouches evoke the mountainous terrain of guerrilla warfare. She flattens close to the ground as the soldiers march by her, then springs up, leaping, circling, slashing out, gathering force like a tornado, then unleashing her weapon at the best target, the last in a column of tired soldiers. She accepts capture and the firing squad with open-armed resignation. The soldiers who pull the trigger lower their heads in silent homage to this courageous woman.

The Young Girl is a passive victim of male exploitation. She stands in a simple yellow frock, kerchief discarded and hair flowing freely, her hands protectively wrapped around her body. The Profiteer brings her to attention and forcefully propels her forward. She is defenseless as one soldier after another picks her up, tosses her and spins around. She lunges in repeated attempts to escape. Totally exhausted, she lies down to rest, but is quickly pulled to her feet again. The brave soldiers who swore allegiance to the flag with idealistic fervor now brutalize a defenseless woman in a brothel.

The Standard Bearer is the epitome of heroic leadership. As the soldiers assemble, his silver helmet gleams and his flag slashes through space in inspired circles and planes. The spring in his heroic step marks the same beat as Death's stationary march. Both are calling up the troops: the one for victory, the other for death. The Standard Bearer embodies all the idealistic illusions of youth: the symbolism of the flag, the shining uniforms, the masculine glory of the fight. In his final entrance the Standard Bearer moves with all his initial fervor, but Death lifts a hand and he falters, his body jerking in convulsive contractions. Several times he tries to go on, but Death thrusts with the flag and the Standard Bearer crumples, drained at last of all illusion.

The scene entitled the Aftermath is a superb moment for Death. Taking possession of the bedraggled, dirty, blood-splattered flag, he leads his victims in a slow processional, each of them frozen in his most characteristic pose. The Old Soldier hangs lifelessly to his arm, one hand still held up swearing eternal fidelity to the flag. After him comes the Partisan, her hands clasped on her chest as they were just before she opened them wide at the moment of her execution. The Old Mother holds a hand to her ear, perpetually listening to the call of death. After her comes a soldier still holding his arms in the posture of the firing squad. He is followed by the Young Girl, her arms open, her head and body bent to the side in eternal exhaustion. The soldier who was killed by the Partisan remains in the posture of a man choked to death. This lamentable group files past with slow halting steps as Death holds the flag aloft with both arms.

Now Death stands in the center and commands the proceedings. The dead revolve in a circle, moving forward and backward with small puppet-like steps. With mechanical motions Death triumphantly lifts and lowers the flag. The dead form a semicircle and Death draws the flag over them in an arc. Like dominoes they crumple to the floor and lie stretched out, as if finally in their graves. Death lowers the flag to the ground like a spear, his legs spread wide and his left hand on his hip. The Standard-Bearer then makes his final entrance, is subdued and joins the ghastly army, the ever-lengthening line of the dead. Once more Death leads this procession across the stage, holding the flag high in the solemn and tragic march which celebrates his victory.

When the Gentlemen in Black reappear and fire their pistols in The Epilogue the cycle has come full circle.

The statement and the message

The Green Table has inspired topical political associations from the very beginning. Jooss mentions some of the early interpretations:

> It was always brought into some kind of relationship to current politics. For instance, when in our first Paris season, in May 1933, all of a sudden, in the applause, they started to shout at us: "A Lausanne, a Lausanne, a Lausanne, a Lausanne!" In Lausanne was the disarmament conference which was completely idle and had gone nowhere. And then, there was always the mistake that people thought the table scenes were the League of Nations. I never meant the League of Nations. I couldn't have meant the League

of Nations, because the war scenes were obviously scenes from
the First World War. The table scene, however, had to be before
the war and at that time there was no League of Nations. I didn't
mean anything specific. I meant that which one doesn't know, but
which somehow exists, these powers which are just to be felt and
not seen. (Huxley, 1982, p.10)

The Green Table is a politically impartial meditation on the senseless
brutality of war. War, regardless of its motivating forces, is an uncontrollable
orgy of death and destruction. It is true that when Jooss choreographed
the ballet he was acutely conscious of the preparations for war that were
being made in heedless defiance of the still-vivid memories of the First World
War. *The Green Table* was a cautionary tale for its day, but the main ideas
of the ballet are of timeless validity. Even today, when war threatens humanity
with global self-annihilation, men are as ready as ever to make preparations
for war.

Jooss made the following statement in 1976:

I am firmly convinced that art should never be political, that art
should not dream of altering people's convictions . . . . I don't
think any war will be shorter or avoided by sending audiences into
The Green Table. (PBS Television, 1982)

Despite Jooss's disclaimer, the ballet is considered a monument to pacifism.
But *The Green Table* is not political propaganda. It does not exhort, instruct
or coerce; it does not label or pass value judgments; it does not take sides.
Jooss presents a series of dramatic events from which the audience must
draw its own conclusions.

The great irony of war is that it is said to be necessary for the sake
of a better life and a safer world, yet it threatens the very existence of both.
Wholesale death and the brutalization of the human spirit are the actual
results of war. The world is not a better place in the final scene, when the
Gentlemen in Black have reassembled at the conference table. Their arguments
are resumed exactly where they left off. On the other hand, perhaps the
eerie silence of their movements during the Epilogue suggests that we have
moved beyond history into a shadow world where Man eternally repeats his
compulsive power games. *The Green Table* is a pacifist ballet that totally
lacks a pacifist agenda, or indeed any agenda at all.

The parallel themes of *The Green Table* cut to the core of man's existence:
his violence and his mortality. Jooss paints a cutting, satirical picture of the
abuse of power. The antics of the Gentlemen in Black show us that grave
consequences are not the monopoly of gross abuses; they flow from small
insincerities, advantage-seeking and manipulative behavior as well. The
Gentlemen in Black make crude threats in moments of anger when the veneer
of etiquette wears thin, but they quickly recover themselves. They do not personally engage in the barbarity of war, but what they unleash upon the world
is the very beast that glared out of their faces in their unguarded moments.

Jooss's impartiality is more damning than any apportionment of blame
would be. The evil cannot be assigned to an army or a cause. It lies deeper
in man: in irrational ways of thinking, fanaticism, greed and aggression.

Death is also a normal part of human existence, of course. It is curious that we think of death as separate from us, a visitation from the outside at the end of our life. In reality we carry death within ourselves from the moment we are born, but we cleverly conceal this from ourselves. The ballet's personification of death gives shape and character to our amorphous notions. This terrifying half-knight and half-skeleton, the elegant mythical monster figure of Death, is a composite of our fearful imaginings.

Nevertheless, Jooss shows us how an individual's own personal character affects his death. Not that life and death are predictable, as if accidents and disease never struck at random. Absurdity is as characteristic of death as it is of life, and the capricious side of existence offers its own provocative material for artistic and philosophical contemplation. But there is still lots of validity in the old saying that he who lives by the sword, dies by the sword. Personal decisions shape our lives, our deaths and the fate of those around us. Jooss's focus on the individual always brings with it a commentary on society as well.

Each person has within himself the potential to live responsibly and to die with dignity. Death seen as apart from us is a part of us as well. At the end his will merges with ours, the presumed duality disappears, and Death becomes one with fate.

A Dance of the Metropolis

Jooss belonged to the generation of artists who matured between the two World Wars. He was a creative participant in the Weimar culture, and like many of his contemporaries he developed a strong social conscience. He had seen the ravages of war and felt emotionally close to the works of Otto Dix, George Grosz and Bertolt Brecht, each of whom dealt in his own way with the resulting social and political ills. He read the works of Kurt Tucholsky who was openly critical of the widespread right-wing militarism. His own work reflected the artistic trend known as *Die Neue Sachlichkeit* or New Objectivity. As its name suggests, the focus of the movement was to observe everyday life and to present it objectively. Humor, irony, caricature and realistic drama were characteristic of the movement, and Jooss used them all.

The Weimar culture was essentially urban in character, and the drama of the metropolis captured the imagination of many artists. This was especially true during the "golden twenties," a time of stability and prosperity when Berlin dominated the cultural scene (Gay, 1968, pp.134–135). The interest in depicting city life coincided with the emergence of *Die Neue Sachlichkeit*. The new realists searched for a clarity and simplicity of expression that would yield an objective view of social issues.

George Grosz drew the people of the city and Bertolt Brecht wrote about them. Fritz Lang produced a film entitled *Metropolis*, and Alfred Doblin's novel *Berlin Alexanderplatz* was made into a movie. The documentary *Berlin – Symphony einer Grosstadt* captured the unique beat of city life. It was the same in the visual arts:

. . . artist after artist reflected the city. Thus Masereel, whose widest public was always in Germany, published *Die Stadt* with Kurt Wolff in 1925, a hundred woodcuts, followed by 112 drawings of *Bilder der Grossstadt* with Carl Reissner the following year, not to mention another laconically-captioned set of urban drawings, *Capitale*, in France after 1933. (Willet, 1978, p.101)

Jooss, who was sensitive to the problems of society and to the times he lived in, created *Big City*. Unlike the many choreographers who dealt with fantasies and fairytales, his subject matter in this ballet was contemporary urban life. He focused on the relationship of the rich and the poor. Wealth and poverty lived side by side in large cities. Since the industrial revolution, the poor from the countryside had flocked to urban areas to work in the factories. Industrial wealth increased the size and prosperity of the leisure class, which stood in contrast to the poverty of the working class.

Big City was considered by many to be the first ballet to deal in social criticism. Jooss himself credits the artists Heinrich Zille and Käthe Kollwitz with inspiration for this work (Program notes, 1974). They painted the life of the proletariat, as did Otto Dix and George Grosz, whose vision and critical beliefs Jooss also shared (Markard & Markard, 1985, p.15). The critic Joachim Schmidt, in a 1982 radio broadcast, said of *Big City*:

> A certain kinship with Brecht is apparent, common elements that stretch from the "myth of the big city" to the analysis of social conditions, which in Jooss's work is as precise as it could be in a nonverbal medium. Where Brecht uses words, Jooss uses movement. For the first time choreography succeeds in expressing social characteristics through dance. In *Big City* the working people of course dance a shuffling waltz, while the rich perform a flashy Charleston: on one hand high-spirited rootless progress, on the other tender solid tradition. (Markard & Markard, 1985, p.11)

Big City was choreographed in 1932. It revolves around the shattered romance of a pair of working class lovers. For the first three years it was danced to Alexandre Tansman's "Sonatine Transatlantique." The music was influenced by American jazz, the Charleston, the Blues and the Foxtrot. In 1935 Tansman composed a new score in which he added, at Jooss's request, a waltz: the French "Bal Musette." The new music was tailored to the existing steps (Program, 1988).

Synopsis of the ballet

BIG CITY

SCENARIO AND CHOREOGRAPHY: Kurt Jooss
MUSIC: Alexandre Tansman, *Sonatine Transatlantique*
       (for two pianos)
COSTUMES: Hein Heckroth

PREMIERE: Cologne Opera, November 21, 1932
ORIGINAL CAST:
     The Young Girl .... Mascha Lidolt
     The Workingman .... Sigurd Leeder
     The Libertine .... Ernst Uthoff
     People on the streets, Mothers, Children ...... The Company

ORDER OF SCENES:
    1.   A Street
    2.   A Working Class District
    3.   The Dance Halls

DURATION: 14 minutes

SCENARIO

The scene is a busy street. As the curtain opens and the music starts, the dancers begin to move. Various characters typical of city life criss-cross the stage in a grid pattern as if crossing a busy intersection. A businessman, a nurse, two gentlemen and a couple of streetwalkers hurry by. A boy is selling newspapers and a girl flowers, both moving with the flow of the crowd. It is late afternoon, a time when some people head for home and others for adventure. A Young Girl is followed by a Young Workingman who has his eye on her. The Libertine who crosses their path is out for adventure.

The costumes are 1920's period outfits.[17] Each character's clothing reveals her status and occupation. In the lead, the Young Girl wears a modest, pale peach, short-sleeved dress with white collar and a belt slung low on her hips. Her hair is put up and on top rests a beret pulled to the side of her head. Demurely, she clutches a small purse to her chest with both hands. The Young Workingman wears beige trousers, shirt, jacket and a cap typical of the working classes of the period. He keeps his hands in his trouser pockets as he moves. The Libertine is in a black coat and tall hat. He wears the social uniform of the upper classes.

Each of the minor characters is a distinct personality and also a member of the anonymous crowd. They pass by each other like strangers, without contact except for a brief friendly gesture to an immediate neighbor. The newspaper boy becomes the focus as he draws attention to his papers. The people who pass by him stop to buy one and begin to read. Then the crowd disperses and only the Young Girl and her admirer remain. They are drawn together in a short duet and we see that they are falling in love. But the Libertine lurks in the shadows. In an opportune moment he steps in and deftly walks off with the Young Girl. Momentarily the street scene resumes and the crowd absorbs them. The people move with an added perkiness; the heightened atmosphere promises adventure. As the lights go out we see the young Workingman left alone, hurt and bewildered.

When the lights come back up, we are in a working class district. Four children, brother-sister pairs, play in a backyard. The boys are in washed out, motley short trousers and the girls wear similar dresses. The game goes sour: a fight breaks out and a little girl begins to cry. The children are absorbed in their own activities until the Young Girl arrives with the Libertine. Then they watch as she accepts a box of gifts and throws herself into his arms with gratitude. She is still in street clothes but he wears a short evening cape with white lining. She runs off with the box and he remains waiting for her.

At this point the two Mothers enter the yard. They are tall strong women, dressed in simple skirt and blouse with hair pulled back in a low bun. They show obvious dislike toward the Libertine, whose presence in the yard is an intrusion and a violation of decency. They act protectively toward their children who view the scene with open curiosity. The Young Girl re-enters wearing the Libertine's gifts: a long white satin dress with a short gray cape matching his. Her hair is loosely combed to her shoulders and she wears silver shoes. She shows off her new outfit, he admires it and whisks her away. As the lights dim the two boys lean forward and with the child's candid innocence slowly extend a finger in a large pointing gesture: just look what they are doing!

The final scene takes place in two dance halls. As the lights come up we see a flashy, feverish, moneyed set. Taxi dancers with their customers, the Libertine and the Young Girl among them, are dancing the Charleston in a modish, angular, cold manner. They are dressed in the glittering flapper outfits of the 1920s. Aquarium green, silver gray and glitter dominate the costumes. The women's short red and blond hair shines in the dim reddish-gold light. The flashy elegance of the costumes suggests the upper classes and the demi-monde. Then the scene gradually changes: out of the darkness at the rear of the stage come four couples dancing the musette. The music first blends Charleston and musette; then, as the Charlestoners fade back into the darkness and disappear, the music becomes pure musette, and we find ourselves in a working-class dance hall with couples dancing slowly in an embrace to mellow romantic music. Our Workingman is there too, but he is alone. The men are in shirts and trousers; the women wear flowered dresses with white collars.

The Young Workingman takes a partner and they perform a brief but spirited virtuoso duet. He has briefly relieved his frustration, but she rejoins her partner and he is alone again. He stands in the center, silent and motionless, as the reverse transition from musette to Charleston takes place: Charlestoners coming forward as the musette dancers fade back and disappear. As the Charleston music reaches full volume, the Workingman also exits.

The Charleston is in full swing. The Libertine, with a smooth turn and a spin, backs into the crowd and vanishes, leaving the Young Girl standing alone. By joining the chorus line the Libertine has become just another anonymous face. The Young Girl rushes off stage. The Young Workingman enters and looks for the Young Girl among the Charleston couples. She makes a final transit across the stage behind him, but they fail to see each other. Their paths fail to cross; their story has ended. The life of the big city goes on as the line of dancers, at the back of the stage, lean sensuously against each other and continue softly stomping out its beat.

The dramatic themes

In *Big City* there are no streets or buildings, only people. But the actions and behavior of these people suggest the atmosphere, the hustle and bustle, and even the physical outlines of the metropolis.

> Inside twenty minutes' action there is etched with fine economy of line the design of the social pattern of the Machine Age city: the life of the Poor and the Bourgeois, the sad and sordid amusements of those who have, and the grayness of the lives of those who have not. (Coton, 1946, p.44)

In the first scene a cheerful urban toughness characterizes the atmosphere. The pace is fast, the air is full of adventure and the people move to the latest jazz rhythms. The street is a busy urban environment where people of all classes and occupations brush past each other. Each person on stage is a distinct individual and at the same time an anonymous member of the city crowd. Their criss-crossing paths seem random and haphazard, but as patterns are repeated the logic and organization of the metropolis emerge.

In the following scenes, elements of social criticism and psychological drama emerge. We see how thoroughly the class structure and its economic ramifications influence the way people live their lives. A critical comparison is made between the disadvantaged condition of the industrial proletariat and the callous, insensitive and immoral attitudes of the wealthy. The story line explores the fragile character of young love, the gullibility of the innocent and the lack of conscience of the sophisticate. The excitements of city life and the allure of urban sophistication are ultimately shown to be rooted in the alienation and the loneliness of the metropolis.

The characters are from the 1920s, possibly from Berlin. The Young Workingman could easily have stepped out of a Brecht poem or play. He wears baggy trousers, a short jacket and a cap; he moves with his hands in his pockets. His sweetheart is a typical working girl, neatly dressed, primly clutching her purse. In a village with traditional values intact, they would marry. But this is an urban story; other forces are at work. The Libertine is a predator looking for adventure and ready and able to pay for it. The Workingman's innocent young girlfriend becomes the prey.

Jooss takes a romantic view of poverty in this piece. His working class district is not a threatening slum but a place where the traditional values survive. Mothers and their children look upon the obvious corruption of the Young Girl with strong disapproval. They know that she could not afford to buy the expensive outfit that she puts on. Her acceptance of the Libertine's gift is the clear indication of her moral degradation. The few moments of confrontation between the Libertine and the Mothers mark an encounter between two deeply antagonistic worlds.

In the first dance hall, characters who could have been sketched by George Grosz or strayed from a scene in *Cabaret* do the high kicks in a Charleston. Dazzled by her finery, eager to please, the Young Girl enthusiastically kicks up her legs. Meanwhile, among the plainly-dressed couples in the proletarian dance hall, the Young Workingman is alone, forlorn and angry. Back among the upper classes, the Libertine disappears into the crowd. His adventure is over and he departs smoothly before any unpleasantness can develop.

The city is big and uncaring: a realm of human opportunities which are quickly lost. At the end the Young Girl searches desperately for the Libertine and for the lost promise of a more glamorous life. The young loner is on a more realistic search for his lost love, but he has delayed too long: their paths do not cross, and they are lost to each other. Their drama proves to be of no significance in the life of the big city; the line of mechanical, emptyfaced Charleston dancers continues to stomp out the rhythms of the Machine Age.

The choreography

In the opening scene each entrance is a small character sketch. The absent-minded businessman plunges into the crowd with large strides. He holds his coat lapels in a stylized gesture; his gaze is on the ground and he almost bumps into people. The nurse, searching for her lost children, hastens across from the other direction. She opens her arms questioningly, then clasps her hands in anguish high on her chest. The flower girl holds out a bunch of flowers in each hand, her arms open in an arc that pleads "please buy." The newspaper boy thrusts his papers forward as he plunges into the crowd, bisecting it on the diagonal. The reading of the city newspaper is a common denominator in which all share in the life of the city. The Young Workingman leans over his sweetheart's shoulder to read her newspaper: a small intimacy familiar to all city-dwellers.

In this street scene thirteen people are on stage. Each person advances from stage right to stage left with an individual step tailored to his character. Upon reaching stage right they all switch into a stylized walk and return on parallel tracks with a uniform sidestep and a gliding conveyor-belt type of locomotion. The individual motifs are resumed upon reaching stage left. At one point everyone stops for an instant and turns to his neighbor in polite greeting. It is a busy crowd, friendly and orderly; the steps are executed smoothly, calmly and noiselessly.

There is a cinematic quality to the choreography of *Big City* that is already evident in the visual impact of the opening scene. The contrasting movement patterns give a bird's eye view of a thoroughfare like New York's Broadway, where a strong diagonal intersects the east-west street grid. Dance critic Marcia Siegel writes:

> I realize it's another one of those times when you have to change your normal orientation drastically, and your visual equipment is not quite the same afterward . . . . : *The Big City* [sic] is not just cinematic, it virtually is a film − a film of the silent and the primal talkies era, when the visual impact had to be strong and immediate and the pacing had to move right along so as not to lose the spectator's presumably tenuous interest. (Siegel, 1977, p.145)

Jooss creates the illusion of two perspectives as if switching between two movie cameras, one with a panoramic view from above and the other at street level. The view from above shows the straight and diagonal network of pathways created by the anonymous moving crowd. The street-level view picks out individuals in the crowd: familiar figures of daily life who emerge for a moment and then blend back into the amorphous masses.

The eccentric hubbub of city life is organized in ways that enable a large population to live orderly lives side by side. The main features of this physical design are the grid and the diagonal. In a remarkable book tracing the development of cities, historian Mark Girouard describes the origins of these design elements:

> For convenience of assigning plots to settlers, the town was laid out on a grid . . . . A web-plan is sensible from the point of view of circulation, but results in shapes between the streets which cannot be divided into standard rectangular lots. Because of this, even new towns with circular walls tended to be laid out as a grid in the Middle Ages; web plans are usually the result of gradual growth. (Girouard, 1985, p.69)

Jooss did not make a systematic study of the sociology of cities, but he instinctively captured their most characteristic design elements in his choreography.

The lead couple are a young man and girl from the slums. Both she and her would-be suitor are heading home from work. The Young Girl walks ahead, looking flirtatiously back over her shoulder. They stand back-to-back looking over their shoulders into each other's eyes. The boy circles the girl with open arms, showing her off: "how beautiful" he seems to say. She slides into a low arabesque, her arms are held aloft, both arms and a leg are suspended in the air in a low turn. He cuddles her in a protective embrace for a second.

When the Young Girl takes the Libertine's arm, ready to abandon the Workingman, he stretches out an arm toward her, calling after her with this gesture. She turns to him, but the Libertine grabs her shoulders, turns her around and plants a quick kiss on her forehead. The Workingman draws back, his frustration and bewilderment showing in his gesture and pose: the slow drag of the foot backward, head lowered, hands in his pockets. When the crowd exits, sweeping along the newly formed couple, the Workingman draws back in angry retreat. Then he lunges and stares after them as the stage goes black.

In the Working Class District, four children are playing in a backyard. They are squatting, holding hands in a circle. The girl who is slapped gets comforted by her friend, who wraps an arm around her shoulders and leads her away. They walk in a bent posture that gives them the appearance of being a child's size. The fight between the two boys is stylized. One threatens the other in a forward lunge with fists clenched at the sides. They bump each other sideways, mock-hit, and fall. The girls return, fascinated by their brothers' rehearsal of manly display. The boys stop fighting, the girls pull them into a circle and the initial game is resumed.

The children are slum brats, but they are nice kids. When they move in a circle they hold themselves very erect; they are clean upright children. They are in deep plie, and jump just high enough to change a foot from back to front. This difficult position and movement simultaneously reduces them to a child's size and gives the impression of a bouncy circle game.

The working-class Mothers are fiercely protective. They enter with long powerful strides. Their hands are on their hips, elbows sharply out to the sides. They cover the stage in gliding sideways steps, one foot crossing over the other; then with a quick directional change they step forward. It is an entrance that emanates control, power and determination. They pull up straight to their full height, chest proudly thrust out. Each mother takes two children, one under each arm, just like a mother hen with her chicks. The two family groups move in unison, advancing with a rhythmic bounce. The kids move away and the brothers and sisters hug, bending low from the waist. The Mothers move from side to side behind the children, arms again spread wide in a protective gesture. Their arms cross in front of their bodies as if warding off an evil spell. They turn, stomp sharply, and gather in their children in protection from the immoral intrusion of the Libertine, making his inappropriate presence in their yard uncomfortable to him.

When the Libertine and the Young Girl enter the yard the children are fascinated. Like little brats they openly stare while scratching imaginary bites, leaning forward and watching every move with intense interest. They break away from their mothers and circle him, slapping their thighs gleefully.

From the moment the Young Girl commits herself to the Libertine, her movements become trance-like as if she had crossed a boundary into another world. As she runs toward him she seems to glide on air. She swoons into his arms; he folds her in his cape and kisses her. The Libertine tips his hat appreciatively when she appears in the expensive evening gown that he has provided; then with a grand gesture he sweeps her off the stage. She casts a brief guilty glance backwards toward the mothers and children. The accusing fingers of the two little boys shoot out from a bent elbow, crossing in front of the body with a childish frankness and naivete that is more damning than the knowing condemnation of the adults. It is a child's gesture that has branded the Young Girl as seduced.

When we are indoors the cinematic quality comes to the fore again in the shifts between two dance halls.

> The overlapping of the dancing scenes is wonderfully and simply done, by having one group gradually move upstage and disappear behind some black drapes, while the other group is coming forward. What makes it look like a movie fadeout is this use of the depth of the stage to make the change, instead of the normal practice of having groups enter and leave at the sides. (Siegel, 1977, p.146)

In the first Dance Hall, couples dance the Charleston with violent hip-swinging sexual energy. It is a syncopated step, and the rhythmically jerking shoulders and sideways bending torsos give the dancers a mechanical quality. Forming two rows, the dancers swing their arms and legs, kicking to the side and high in front as they travel from side to side. Their efforts convey their selfconscious abandon to entertainment.

In contrast, the couples of the other Dance Hall are a subdued, sentimental lot. The musette is a slow twostep waltz that looks simpler than it is, combining a long sliding step with a turning step. The partners stand huddled together and hold each other close; the tone is intimate and romantic.

The Libertine's movements are those of an experienced predator: oiled and smooth. When he first stalks his prey he glides by the young couple, taking note of the girl's good looks. Then he boldly leaps between them, taking advantage of a momentary physical separation. He struts and preens. His hat is already off to greet her; he puts it back on pompously with two hands and offers his arm to her. Flattered, she takes it; he points the way and they begin to walk with an elegant pattern of larger and smaller steps. It is like a conversation: small talk of the feet. His movements are full of upper class mannerisms. When the children surround him in the courtyard he stands aloof, defiantly wrapped in his cape. He pulls himself up as if their smell, the odor of the slums, bothers him. When the Mothers approach him challengingly, he flicks his cape and adjusts his gloves arrogantly, trying to be rid of them. In the Dance Hall his partnering of the Young Girl is deft, and his disappearance by merging into the line of Charleston dancers is smooth. A quick and complete betrayal is accomplished with clever ease in a few steps.

Behind the Young Workingman, vainly looking for her among the Charleston dancers, the Young Girl runs across the stage, still searching. Desperately she follows a large zigzag pattern but fails to cross his line of vision. She disappears while he is turned in the wrong direction, gazing glumly into empty space. The line of anonymous Charleston dancers has retreated to the background where they continue to move in place: the beat goes on.

The statement and the message

Big City tells a typical urban story. It is fast-paced and descriptive, setting forth the life and atmosphere of the city, its social realities and its class structure. The story chronicles the temptations of city life and the glitter of the fast track. It also reflects the alienation and the loneliness that so often exist beneath the surface of the bustling crowd.

The ballet is a period piece in the sense that it depicts the Metropolis of the 1920's: the jazz age, the age of the urban proletariat, the machine age. Like all cities, it is a place that echoes with individual laughter and tears, while from another perspective the individual is just another face in the crowd. The tragedy which leaves a person devastated is not even noticed and leaves no mark on the city; life goes on as before. The individual is brought into sharp relief for a moment, then blends into the general crowd. This is the bright hard rhythm and beat of the city, an existence that is ultimately without mercy and without regard for the individual's longings and losses.

In *Big City* Jooss shows how a person's individuality is also expressive of the patterns of the collective. His individuality lights up in his personal struggles, his vulnerabilities and aspirations. At the same time his story is the unfolding of the consequences of the environing social organization and class structure. In the urban setting he achieves an anonymity which at once heightens his sense of individual adventure and gives license to irresponsibility and indifference.

In *Big City* Jooss shows us the fragility of young love, the pain of betrayal and the loneliness that follows abandonment. We see exploitation between the classes and between the sexes. But we see all this as the flip side of the energizing and exciting dynamics of city life. Rarely has so real a tragedy been set in so cheerful and alluring a framework as Jooss has done in this ballet.

A Social Dance

A Ball in Old Vienna is a lighthearted humorous ballet choreographed to Josef Lanner's *Hofballtanze*. The costumes, designed by Jooss's wife Aino Siimola, suggest that the ball takes place in the epoch when the music was composed, the 1840's. Both Jooss and his wife were accomplished ballroom dancers, and the ballet was inspired by their love of the waltz. They researched the different kinds of waltzes, and the choreography includes many of them. Häger reports:

> This knowledge he used in *A Ball in Old Vienna*, and his great musicality as well. It is seemingly a bagatelle, a light entertainment for the public in between the perturbing tragic ones. But Jooss had a serious purpose as well, he wanted to create a "depot" for all known forms of waltzes, the ones his wife Aino knew from Russia, and the original ones dating back to his own grandmother and the flowering of the waltz. (Häger, in press, p.15)

The waltz is one of the oldest social dance forms still practiced today. Its origin has been traced to the middle of the 18th century, to southern Germany. Musicologist and dance historian Curt Sachs has identified its predecessors as the Bavarian folk dances called *Ländlers*. These were turning and jumping dances done in a moderate tempo by the villagers of that rugged mountain terrain. Later the tempo became faster on the smooth ballroom floor,

> but by and large the waltz remained the same as the *Ländler*: a three-four rhythm with a strong accent on the first beat, to each two measures of which the couples in close embrace make a turn and at the same time follow a circular course, so that the dance resembles the two-fold rotation of the heavenly bodies; the left foot strides out, the right follows gliding in a backward curve, and the left completes the half circle. In the second measure the same figure [in a backward step] is repeated with the right foot leading. (Sachs, 1963, pp.429–430)

The turning and spinning of the waltz may have reminded the romantics of the revolution of heavenly bodies, but it carried a less exalted connotation for the bourgeoisie. The close proximity of the dancing couples and the rapid swirling turns were considered indecent and dangerous. While young poets called the waltz intoxicating, rapturous, thrilling and ecstatic, the older generation found it excessive and warned of its harmful effects. As late as the early 20th century, during the rule of Kaiser Wilhelm II, the waltz was forbidden at imperial balls (Sachs, 1963, p.431). In spite of such objections the waltz spread rapidly, and by the end of the 18th century its many varieties had become the rage all over Europe. Soon it crossed the Atlantic and continued to evolve in America.

In *The Dance Encyclopedia* the waltz is described as follows:

> Ballroom dance in 3/4 time, of which there are two basic variations: the faster Viennese waltz, in which couples turn in circles in one direction, and the slower Boston (originated in America), in which the couples turn in circles in several directions. (Chujoy & Manchester, 1967, p.958)

Several additional varieties of the waltz were developed: a skipping version in France; the Hesitation Waltz invented by Vernon and Irene Castle; a Scottish variety; a two-step variation in Germany.

> The classical form, however, is and remains the Viennese waltz, which on the Danube was called the *Langaus* . . . . In the Viennese waltz we have that overemphasis of the first beat and underemphasis of the second and at the same time that transparent floating and gliding which is suited to the lightness of urban dance dress and the smoothness of the floor. The urban influence makes itself felt also in the melodic line; the extreme leaps and wide intervals give place more and more to smooth progression − dance and music alike tend toward close movement. Finally we have a change of form; with the great increase in tempo the old familiar eight-measure period of the *Ländler* and the German waltz were altogether too short and were extended to sixteen measures. This development did not come about at all suddenly. Even Josef Lanner calls his dances *Ländler* or *Deutsche* first; not until his Opus 7 does he use the title waltz, and then not throughout. (Sachs, 1963, pp.433−434)

In addition to his most serious artistic intentions, Jooss was a true artist of the theater. He was proud of being an entertainer and took his responsibilities to the public very seriously. He handled every aspect of his productions with great professionalism. When he put together the program for "Ballets Jooss" in 1932, he placed *Ball* just before the intermission so that the audience would go out in a cheerful mood.[18] This was a good choice, for there is, as A. V. Coton put it, "a delicacy, a fluency and an air of youthfulness about this ballet" that can not fail to amuse.

Synopsis of the ballet

A BALL IN OLD VIENNA

SCENARIO AND CHOREOGRAPHY: Kurt Jooss
MUSIC: *Hofballtänze*, Josef Lanner
          Arranged for two pianos by F. A. Cohen
COSTUMES: Aino Siimola
PREMIERE: Cologne Opera, November 21, 1932
ORIGINAL CAST:

The Debutante	Lisa Czobel
Her Admirer	Werner Stemmer
Her Aunts	Lola Botka, Masha Lidolt
The Eligible Young Man	Ernst Uthoff
(later renamed The Baron)	
His Sweetheart	Elsa Kahl
The Dancing Master	Karl Bergeest
His Partner	Frida Holst
Dancing Couples	Edgar Frank, Ruth Harris,
	Maria Kindlova, Heinz Rosen

DURATION: 10 minutes

SCENARIO

The short overture is played and the curtain rises. The stage is dark, then suddenly flooded in bright light. A brilliant chandelier hangs center stage. In the opening tableau all participants are on stage. The ladies are in various arrested poses center stage, and the men stand on the periphery: it is a moment frozen in time. The costumes are spectacular. The ladies are in long white dresses with skirts of many layers of ruffled starched silk organza. These are attached to a tight bodice with puffed sleeves and a ruffled decolletage. Curls and flowers frame their heads. The gentlemen wear tails in several shades of blue and gray, tan trousers, white ruffled shirts and white gloves. They sport long sideburns.

When the tableau breaks, the Dancing Master leads the ladies in a sweeping run around the stage, with the two Aunts chaperoning the Debutante. The old ladies' costume is identical to the young girls' except that its color is light gray, matching their graying curls; a thin black ribbon is worn on the neck. The gentlemen politely stand to the side, watching the ladies. The Dancing Master is center stage, ready to give the first lesson. He elegantly demonstrates a figure, and the two Aunts are the first to try it. Then all the ladies do it in unison and the gentlemen applaud. Then the gentlemen follow the Baron in a little extravaganza, another waltz.

The Aunts notice that the Debutante is dancing with a young boy, her admirer. They pull her away from him and present her to their own choice, the handsome Baron. He dazzles and bewilders her. She becomes shy and her dancing turns absurdly awkward. He gives up on her after one spin, leaves her, and returns to the lady of his choice. The Debutante sits down rejected and both she and her Aunts cry. The Aunts rush off in despair. But the Young Admirer, who has been watching from the sidelines, returns and asks her to dance, and in his arms she suddenly becomes graceful. The other couples are promenading around. The Aunts, hoping to remedy the situation, try to separate the couple but do not succeed.

The Baron and his Sweetheart find themselves alone for a moment and they embrace. But the Aunts come in and with grave disapproval point a forbidding finger at her. She is not intimidated by the old ladies; on the contrary, she asserts her position by a demonstrative duet with her partner. The Aunts are moping. All the guests come in, link arms and shoo the Aunts away.

The Dancing Master leads his partner forward. She demonstrates a special step for the ladies, who all follow. Then the ladies sit, their white dresses shimmering like snowflakes. They passively exhibit their beauty, as was the custom, waiting for the men to come and greet them. They do so, amidst an exchange of pleasantries and congratulations.

The Dancing Master once again claps for attention and demonstrates an elegant little step, his own invention. Everyone follows obediently. The Baron and his Sweetheart dance together, while the Debutante and her Admirer stand in deep conversation. As they begin to dance the rest form a protective line behind them.

A new mood takes hold, creating a swirling ballroom atmosphere. Everyone is dancing in sweeping circles that gradually widen. The men hold hands in a circle and the ladies sit on their interlocked arms facing outward. In this formation the group revolves like a merry-go-round made of white roses. The ladies pose in a tableau as they are deposited on the floor once again in a circle. The men form a bigger circle around them. As if playing a child's game the ladies run out to them, then turn back to their own circle.

After the waltz of the grand finale, all assemble in a final tableau. The Aunts run in and execute a low curtsey; the ladies bow and the gentlemen bend low from the waist to kiss their hands. During the inevitable wild applause, the Dancing Master turns questioningly to his partner, who assents to an encore. He turns around and with an exaggerated bow gives the sign to begin again. The entire concluding sequence is then repeated, beginning with the spectacular merry-go-round scene.

The dramatic themes

A Ball in Old Vienna is a comedy of manners, lightly satirical in tone and spectacular in its visual beauty. It makes good-natured fun of the behavior of Viennese high society, satirizing its refined elegance and self-important irrelevance. It is a tongue-in-cheek but loving caricature of an insular but harmless society, a society slightly decadent but untouched by the horrors of world wars. Marcia Siegel says:

> Its subject, I think, is the attractiveness of a society that works in harmonious organized patterns . . . . Secure in their community's well understood design, they're also free to be individuals. (Siegel, 1977, p.148)

They are also free to rebel, but within understood limits, the young defying their elders in matters of the heart.

The satire is exemplified by the character of the two maiden aunts and their all-too-obvious manipulations to pair off their charge with the right suitor. They act in unison, glancing at one another knowingly like conspirators with a prepared course of action. When noting that the Debutante is dancing with the ''wrong'' partner, they throw up their arms in alarm and make a bee-line for her from opposite sides of the stage. Moving her partner out of the way, they take her by the hands and fussily present her to the intended beau. When their efforts have failed they walk away in a moping posture, torso bent parallel to the floor, skirts held out in front.

Later, when the Aunts see The Baron embracing his Sweetheart, they walk right up to the couple, hitch up their voluminous skirts with one hand and point a finger with outstretched arm. They shake their heads disapprovingly; then, stepping closer, they try to shoo her away with open palms. Between episodes of frustrated humiliation and recovered pride they participate gaily in the ball, joining in the large waltzing scenes. They are fervent admirers of the Dancing Master and are eager to follow his instructions and try his steps.

The Dancing Master is the figure of authority, slightly comical in his exaggerated vanity and somewhat fussy. He claps his hands to call attention to himself, then demonstrates a step with refined elegance and well chosen precision. he bows from the waist and leads the ladies with just the correct flourish. Even with his exaggerated manners he is the obvious epitome of the current standards of sophistication. Elderly aunts and young ladies alike gaze at him adoringly. He plays hard to get, and the women beg him with fervently clasped hands to demonstrate his superb mastery of the waltz.

Ball has the atmosphere of a Viennese operetta, where intrigue is overcome by true love, a few tears are quickly exchanged for laughter, and the story line is a sketch that gets filled in by the beauty of the music and the dance.

The choreography

In *Ball* Jooss comes closest to abstract dance. Its revolving circular patterns, powerful diagonals and starbursts of leaping, twirling dancers present a glorious sight. The tableau of reclining maidens, their skirts spread around them like flower petals, is a lovely sight. The gentlemen, forming an outstretched line as they lean over them to kiss their hands, are the epitome of Old World manners.

The imaginative and expressive use of the waltz is the basis of this ballet. Waltz steps are interspersed with classical combinations and expressive movement. The few connecting steps and gestures serve to advance the story. The leaps of the men and the diagonal and circular group formations and floor patterns add to the visual excitement. The many forms of the waltz are made to look simple and effortless, though in fact they are intricate and difficult to perform.

The waltzes in the ballet include material discovered through research by Jooss as well as his own elaboration on these findings. The story is told by different kinds of steps and rhythmic patterns. Each waltz has a different accent. The mood is set by a ''jumped'' waltz. The ''dotted'' waltz has a clipped rhythm accented on the third beat. The Boston waltz has a sliding, gliding quality with the accent on the second beat; the Polish waltz consists entirely of jumps with the accent on the first beat. There is also a waltz with a cabriole or small beat of the feet, and a waltz where the foot performs a small kick in the back. There is a ''peasant mazurka,'' a waltz-mazurka and a Russian waltz.

In one waltz pattern the men lift the women off the floor to the accent of the music as the women execute a scissor-kick in the air with their legs. Upon landing, they waltz and turn in place, holding the outstretched hand of their partner. All this is done with an even flow, gliding smoothly over the ground. In another pattern the ladies waltz in a circle with large circling leg lifts or développés. Starting counterclockwise, they reverse direction and rotate clockwise. The ordered symmetry of such choreographic devices enhances the visual beauty of the ballet. In another pleasing pattern the couples change partners, each lady overtaking the gentleman ahead of her. As the circle of couples revolves, within it each couple rotates in smaller circles.

At one point the ladies seat themselves in a row across the stage, and the gentlemen leap through the gaps between them with a grand jeté. With the large frilly skirts of the women spread out for background, this collective leap looks like a starburst. Facing outward, the women hold their dresses and waltz in a circle, closing and opening the folds of their dresses with a swirl and a swish, adding width and breadth to their dimensions. The choreographic patterns of the ballet are built on these contrasts and harmonies of circles and lines in space.

The most spectacular scene in the ballet is the ''merry-go-round:'' the revolving circle of women sitting on the arms of the men. This formation mirrors the only scenery, the multi-tiered brass chandelier with white candle bowls. The sparkle of its light is reflected in the shimmer of the ruffled costumes. The smoothly flowing, gliding quality of the waltz, with its swirling turns and its circles upon rotating circles floating by, creates a soothing and at the same time exhilarating harmony.

The best example of the expressively communicative use of the waltz is when the Debutante dances with the Baron. She suddenly becomes awkward, and her body leans horizontally as her chest slides down nearly to her partner's waist. Her neck is stretched out and her upthrust chin is glued to the front of her partner's ruffled shirt. Her legs kick out in the back with each waltzing step, making her look like a clumsy duckling paddling desperately to stay afloat. Obviously the two are incompatible, totally unsuited to each other. The Baron's Sweetheart glides effortlessly into his arms and they waltz away with elegant ease. The Debutante then dances with her Admirer and her awkwardness disappears, their movements graceful and complementary.

The statement and the message

Ball is a whimsical piece, the icing on the cake of an evening's program. In its treatment it exhibits some nostalgia for a bygone era, the carefree

Viennese society where life revolved around dancing lessons and suitors. The generation gap existed and the older generation tried to impose its will on the younger one, but the gap implied no stress or alienation. Both sides recognized the inevitability of conflict and accepted the time-honored devices for blunting or evading it with humor and good grace. The ballet makes innocent fun of silly behavior while at the same time capturing the flavor of its charm.

A Ball in Old Vienna is pure entertainment: sparkling in beauty, exhilarating and amusing. What message it has is largely incidental to its formal beauty. Jooss's natural propensity as a story-teller led him to place his presentation of the many varieties of the waltz within a dramatic context. He drew a mild caricature of an era and a society through its most characteristic social dance. Without this context the ballet would be a series of exhibition ballroom dances; within it, it is a work of art.

Notes

1. Laban dropped the "von" from his name in the 1940's and referred to himself from then on plainly as Rudolf Laban. But Jooss always thought of him as "von Laban."
2. Laban himself alternately refers to this work as a "play" and as "pure dance", suggesting that Jooss's dramatic abilities made up for his lack of technical proficiency.
3. Manuscript in the Elsa Kahl Cohen archives.
4. Personal notes of Elsa Kahl Cohen, in the author's possession.
5. As the oldest son, F. A. Cohen had taken over the running of the family publishing house after his father died.
6. In Teutonic mythology *Folkwang* was the banquet hall of Freya, the goddess of love and beauty. It was located in a great meadow in the sky where heroes were invited to be her guests. The owner of the paintings who donated them for the establishment of the Essen museum chose the name because he intended the museum to be a place where people met to be inspired by creativity.
7. This system of notation was first published in 1956, during Laban's lifetime. It was first presented to the public in 1928, during the Dance Congress in Essen.
8. Personal communication from Elsa Kahl Cohen, January 1988. Elsa Cohen appeared among the Ladies of the Court in the original production of this work.
9. During a conversation with F. A. Cohen about Ravel's piano piece, Jooss asked the question: "What caused the death of the Infanta?" The ballet constitutes the answer to his own question (Personal communication with Anna Markard, June 1988).
10. From the Jooss Master File of the Dance Notation Bureau. The German text is: ingeschnurt in den Zwang des kalten und bombastischen Hofzeremonielles (symbolisiert durch das Schrittmotiv der Pavane) sucht die junge Infantin vergeblich, sich zu befreien und unterliegt am Ende der Burde der unveränderlichen Etikette.
    Originally Jooss had three Ladies of the Court. But the symmetry created by the equal number of dancers on the two sides was too obvious, and soon after the premiere he added two more dancers (personal communication with Anna Markard, March 1988). In all of the productions that this author has studied, the number of Ladies has been five.
11. The first description of the pavane can be found in Thoinot Arbeau's 1588 *Orchesography* (Arbeau, 1969, pp. 57–59).

12. Information on the premiere comes from the Jooss Master File of the Dance Notation Bureau. The original cast is listed in the program notes for a performance by the Essen Opera Ballet on June 10, 1988, celebrating the 50th anniversary of the Second Dance Congress in Essen, organized by Jooss. The 1988 program was entitled *Ballet Jooss '32*.

13. Even today, cellophane is sewn into the panels of the skirts to give a special characteristic rustle, even though it is now hard to obtain cellophane because plastics have replaced it for most uses (personal communication with Anna Markard, September 1988).

14. Jooss declared: "I have said everything I wanted to say." He considered economy of expression to be an important virtue (personal communication with Anna Markard, June 1988).

15. The interviews referred to here were conducted by Tobi Tobias, John Gruen and Walter Terry. The interview with Michael Huxley was conducted as a part of a doctoral research project at the University of Leeds, England. A transcript appeared in *Ballett International* on the fiftieth anniversary of the ballet's premiere (Huxley, 1982, pp.8–12).

16. Photographs of the masks exist and are printed in A. V. Coton, *The New Ballet*, p.88.

17. The original costumes for the Charleston were Spanish. In Germany in the 1920's, the Charleston was associated with Spanish dancing. In 1950 Jooss renamed the ballet *Big City*, *1926* and it was performed under this title for two years before reverting to the original (Personal communication with Anna Markard, January 1984).

18. Personal communication with Anna Markard, June 1988.

Figure 1. Portrait of Kurt Jooss (1935 or 1936). Photo: Gordon Anthony, London.
Dance Collection, The New York Public Library for the Performing Arts, Astor, Lenox and
Tilden Foundations.

Figure 2. *Dance of Death in '17: Dead Man Hill* (1924). Etching by Otto Dix.
From the portfolio *War.* II/9. Berlin, Karl Nierendorf.
Collection, The Museum of Modern Art, New York, Abby Aldrich Rockefeller Fund.

Figure 3. *God for Us* (1919). Lithograph by George Grosz.
Plate I from the portfolio *God for Us*. Berlin, Der Malik-Verlag, 1920.
Collection, The Museum of Modern Art, New York, Abby Aldrich Rockefeller Fund.

Figure 4. *War Cripples* (1920). Drypoint by Otto Dix.
Collection, The Museum of Modern Art, New York, Purchase Fund.

Figure 5. *The Germans to the Front* (1919). Lithograph by George Grosz.
Plate II from the portfolio *God for Us*. Berlin, Der Malik-Verlag, 1920.
Collection, The Museum of Modern Art, New York, Abby Aldrich Rockefeller Fund.

Figure 6. *Death Seizing a Woman* (1934). Lithograph by Käthe Kollwitz.
Plate IV from the series *Death*. Collection, The Museum of Modern Art, New York, Purchase Fund.

Figure 7. *The Call of Death* (1934–35). Lithograph by Käthe Kollwitz.
Plate VIII from the series *Death*. Collection, The Museum of Modern Art, New York, Purchase Fund.

Figure 8. Infanta with Ladies of the Court (1992).
Pavane on the Death of an Infanta, Kurt Jooss, 1929. Ballet du Rhin.
Infanta: Sandrine Moreau. Photo: Laurent Philippe. The Jooss Archives.

Figure 9. Infanta with the Court (n.d.). *Pavane on the Death of an Infanta*, Kurt Jooss, 1929. Deutsche Oper Berlin. Infanta: Dianne Bell. Photo: Buhs/Remler. The Jooss Archives.

Figure 10. Street Scene I (1935–36). *Big City*, Kurt Jooss, 1932. Ballets Jooss. Libertine: Ernst Uthoff, Workingman: Hans Züllig, Young Girl: Noelle de Mosa. Photo: Gordon Anthony, London. Dance Collection, The New York Public Library for the Performing Arts, Astor, Lenox and Tilden Foundations.

Figure 11. Street Scene II (1978). *Big City*, Kurt Jooss, 1932. Het Nationale Ballet Amsterdam, Young Girl: Mea Venema, Workingman: Hans Zullig, Libertine: Francis Sinceretti. The Jooss Archives.

Figure 12. The Workers Quarters (1937). *Big City*, Kurt Jooss, 1932. Ballets Jooss on tour, Budapest, Young Girl: Noelle de Mosa, Libertine: Ernst Uthoff. Photo: Pecsi. The Jooss Archives.

Figure 13. Waltz (1935). *A Ball in Old Vienna*, Kurt Jooss, 1932. Ballets Jooss, London, The Debutante: Noelle de Mosa, Her Admirer: Hans Züllig. Photo: Gordon Anthony, London. The Jooss Archives.

Figure 14. Group Scene (1935–36). *A Ball in Old Vienna*, Kurt Jooss, 1932. Ballets Jooss. Photo: Gordon Anthony, London. The Jooss Archives.

Figure 15. *Lübecker Totentanz* (1701). Fresco in the Marienkirche at Lübeck.
Dance Collection, The New York Public Library for the Performing Arts, Astor, Lenox and
Tilden Foundations.

Ensign, surrender at my call,
Or direst harm shall thee befall!
Thy colours bright must be my prize,
Whilst o'er thy corpse Death's banner flies.

Enfin, je t'ai mon beau vaillant!
·J'arrache ta chère bannière
Elle flottera bien plus fière
Enseigne, sur ton corps sanglant!

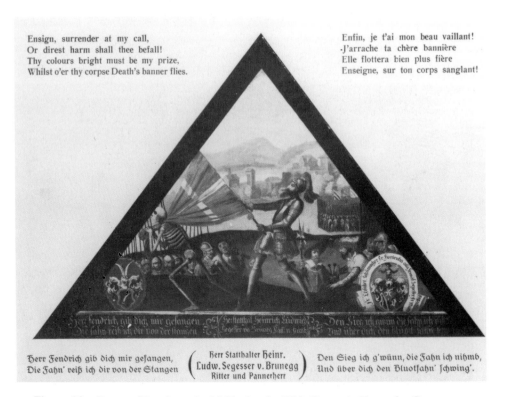

Herr Fendrich gib dich mir gefangen,
Die Fahn' reiß ich dir von der Stangen

Herr Statthalter Heinr.
Ludw. Segesser v. Brunegg
Ritter und Pannerherr

Den Sieg ich g'wünn, die Fahn ich nihmb,
Und über dich den Bluotfahn' schwing'.

Figure 16. *Dance of Death on the Muhlenbrücke* (17th Century). Fresco by Caspar von
Meglinger in the Church of the Spreuerbrücke at Lucerne, Switzerland. Dance Collection,
The New York Public Library for the Performing Arts, Astor, Lenox and Tilden Foundations.

Tafel 10. Der Tod und die Jungfrau.

Figure 17. *Death and the Maiden* (early woodcut). Dance Collection,
The New York Public Library for the Performing Arts, Astor, Lenox and Tilden Foundations.

Figure 18. *Dance of Death* (17th Century). Fresco by Caspar von Meglinger in the Church of the Spreuerbrücke at Lucerne, Switzerland. Dance Collection, The New York Public Library for the Performing Arts, Astor, Lenox and Tilden Foundations.

Figure 19. The Gentlemen in Black I (1932). *The Green Table*, Kurt Jooss, 1932. Ballets Jooss. Photo: Renger-Patzsch. The Jooss Archives.

Figure 20. The Gentlemen in Black II (1935–36). *The Green Table*, Kurt Jooss, 1932.
Ballets Jooss. Photo: Gordon Anthony, London. Dance Collection,
The New York Public Library for the Performing Arts, Astor, Lenox and Tilden Foundations.

Figure 21. Death's Solo (1985). *The Green Table*, Kurt Jooss, 1932.
Essen Ballet, Death: Christian Holder. Photo: Armin Wenzel. The Jooss Archives.

Figure 22. The Farewells (1932). *The Green Table*, Kurt Jooss, 1932.
Ballets Jooss, Soldiers: Ernst Uthoff, Hans Züllig, Young Girl: Noelle de Mosa.
Posed photo: Sacha, London. Dance Collection, The New York Public Library for the
Performing Arts, Astor, Lenox and Tilden Foundations.

Figure 23. The Battle I (1991). *The Green Table*, Kurt Jooss, 1932.
Ballet de Rhin, Soldiers: Alain Imbert, Sylvain Boulet. The Jooss Archives.

Figure 24. The Battle II (1951). *The Green Table*, Kurt Jooss, 1932.
Folkwang Tanztheater/Ballets Jooss, Profiteer: Alfonso Unanue.
Photo: Patrician Pictures, Amsterdam. The Jooss Archives.

Figure 25. The Battle III (1977). *The Green Table*, Kurt Jooss, 1932.
Deutsche Oper Berlin, Profiteer: Vladimir Gelvan. Photo: Krapich Photo. The Jooss Archives.

Figure 26. The Refugees (1960's). *The Green Table*, Kurt Jooss, 1932.
Folkwangballett, Old Mother: Pina Bausch. Photo: Anthony Crickmay. The Jooss Archives.

Figure 27. The Brothel (1978). *The Green Table*, Kurt Jooss, 1932.
National Ballet Amsterdam, Soldier: Leo Besseling, Young Girl: Mea Venema.
Photo: Jorge Fatauros. The Jooss Archives.

Figure 28. The Aftermath (1932). *The Green Table*, Kurt Jooss, 1932. Ballet Jooss, Death: Kurt Jooss, The Old Soldier: Rudolf Pescht. Photo: Lipnitzki. The Jooss Archives.

Figure 29. Soldiers (1935). *The Mirror*, Kurt Jooss, 1935. Ballets Jooss. The Jooss Archives.

Figure 30. Prisoners (1952). *Journey in the Fog,* Kurt Jooss, 1952.
Folkwang Tanztheater/Ballets Jooss, Prisoners: Patricio Brunster, Alfonso Unanue.
Photo: d'Hooghe. The Jooss Archives.

Figure 31. Portrait of Kurt Jooss (Köln, 1976). Photo: Gert Weigelt. The Jooss Archives.

CHAPTER IV: THE JOOSS LEGACY

Jooss's Later Years

In 1933 Jooss was forced to flee Nazi Germany. In that year a German newspaper published an article with this lengthy and ominous title: "The Truthful Jacob, KURT JOOSS AS MOSES' TEMPLE DANCER: Without Cohen the Jew He Cannot Fulfill his Artistic Mission." Jooss personally went to the headquarters of the Nazi Party to protest their demand that he dismiss the Jewish members of his company (Markard & Markard, 1985, p.51). His uncompromising attitude led the Nazis to escalate their rhetoric, and the *Ballets Jooss* was accused of harboring not only Jews, but also Kultur-Bolsheviks and homosexuals. Jooss had exposed himself to great danger, and was warned by the Freemasons that his arrest was imminent. An escape was arranged and Jooss fled to Holland with the entire company. These events brought to a sudden end the most creative phase of Jooss's career.

After the flight from Nazi Germany, while the Ballets Jooss was on tour through Europe and America, Jooss received an invitation from a wealthy British couple, Leonard and Dorothy Elmhirst, to bring his school to England (Markard & Markard, 1985, p.55). Thus began a new chapter in Jooss's life and career. In April of 1934 his school reopened at Dartington Hall in Devon, England, under the name "Jooss-Leeder School of Dance."

In September 1935, the Ballets Jooss was also reestablished at Dartington hall (Markard & Markard, 1985, p.55). A core group of dancers from the original company was joined by pupils of the school. Jooss's first addition to their repertory was a sequel to *The Green Table* entitled *The Mirror*.

This ballet was also a collaboration between Jooss, F. A. Cohen and Hein Heckroth. Where *The Green Table* focused on the figure of Death and his victims, *The Mirror* showed the survivors of war. The work "reflects the confusion and worries, the despair and the hopes of post-war mankind struggling to escape from the moral, social and political consequences of his own folly" (Coton, 1946, p.59). The scenario focused on the grim realities of post-war civilian existence.

Much later, after his return to Germany, Jooss choreographed a third ballet on the theme of war. *Journey in the Fog* was inspired by his personal experiences during the Second World War. It consisted of four scenes, each reflecting on a different aspect of hardship and suffering: "the loneliness

of exile; the claustrophobia of internment in camp; the shadow of
bereavement; and the restlessness of attempted rehabilitation'' (Häger, in
press). *Green Table, Mirror* and *Fog* form a trilogy dealing with the gravest
events of our twentieth century, the century shaped by global warfare. It
is deeply disappointing that only the first of these ballets has survived.

In 1939 Jooss choreographed *Chronica*, a full length ballet dealing with
another timely topic: the horrors of dictatorship. His portrayal of a medieval
despot and the suffering he inflicts on his subjects made allegorical reference
to Hitler and Germany. With the entire new repertory, the Ballets Jooss
travelled to the United States in 1940 for an extensive tour, including a long
engagement in New York City.

Jooss had remained in England, expecting to devote his time to the Jooss-
Leeder School. However, England adopted the wartime policy of evacuating
aliens from the coastal areas of England, and the school was forced to close.
Jooss, as a German national, was interned as an ''enemy alien'' (Markard
& Markard, 1985, p.59). This was a devastating experience for him, although
he kept his spirits high. As related by fellow inmate Robert Ziller:

> In camp he [Jooss] was wonderful. His courage and his patience
> inspired us all. He never ceased to tell us that England couldn't
> help herself, and that we who are her friends must understand
> that and be patient. But in his heart he is very unhappy. (Markard
> & Markard, 1985, p.61)

Jooss's wife Aino Siimola worked relentlessly for his release. He was freed
after six months, following the intervention of some prominent intellectuals.

The *Ballets Jooss* was reestablished for the third time in Cambridge in
1942. Again Jooss added a new work to the company's repertory that was
visionary for its time, entitled *Pandora*. Häger describes this ballet as ''deeply
disturbing.'' He writes:

> Refraining from his customary clarity of message, he created visions
> of future dangers for humanity, warning against unrestrained
> curiosity and ingenuity. It was as if he had a presentiment of the
> atom bomb a year before it happened, and of the evils to follow
> in its wake. (Häger, in press)

The new repertory of Ballets Jooss premiered at The Haymarket in London
two days before D-Day in June 1944. It was not until 1947 that Jooss was
finally granted British citizenship.

The final phase of Jooss's career began with an invitation from the
Folkwangschule in Essen to return as Director of the Dance Division once
again. He was also offered a subsidy from the municipality of Essen for
a new dance company. He accepted, and in 1949, with great hopes for the
future, he returned to Germany for good.

In his remaining years Jooss pursued his mission as an educator, working
at the Folkwangschule and teaching in summer schools in Switzerland. From
1954 to 1956 he directed the Düsseldorf Opera with the hope of establishing
a *Tanztheater* there. The administration had promised help in the founding
of an independent dance company. He resigned his position when this help

failed to materialize.

During the next few years Jooss travelled in Europe teaching and choreographing. In Essen he established a Master's Program for Dance under the name of *Folkwang Dance Studio*. The students in these classes were given opportunities to choreograph and to perform. From these Master Classes evolved Jooss's last company, the *Folkwangballet*. In addition to Jooss's choreography, the repertory included works by other distinguished artists such as Anthony Tudor's *The Lilac Garden*, Jean Cebron's *Struktur, Sequence, Recueil,* and Lucas Hoving's *Songs of Encounter* and *Icarus*. Pina Bausch's first effort in choreography, *Fragment*, was also included in the program.

Jooss retired from his post at the Folkwangschule in 1968. He continued to work as a guest choreographer, and occasionally restaged his ballets for dance companies and art festivals. In 1972 he delegated the responsibility for restaging the original Ballets Jooss program to his daughter Anna Markard, who continues to set these ballets, most importantly *The Green Table*, for dance companies all over the world.

Jooss lost his wife Siimola in 1971. It was a great blow to him, for she had been his lifetime companion and his most trusted artistic adviser. He moved from Essen to Kreuth in Bavaria, where he spent the rest of his life. Jooss died in 1979 in Heilbronn, from injuries sustained in an automobile accident.

In 1976, in celebration of Jooss's seventy-fifth birthday, Robert Joffrey revived the original Ballets Jooss program at the City Center 55th Street Theater. These four ballets – *Big City*, *Pavane on the Death of an Infanta*, *A Ball in Old Vienna*, and *The Green Table* – are all that remain of the forty to fifty ballets that Jooss choreographed in his lifetime. Appropriately, their survival owes much to Labanotation, which in turn owes a great deal to Jooss.

Jooss's artistic legacy goes far beyond those four ballets. He pioneered an approach to dance expression in which content determines form and technique is the direct outcome of dramatic necessity. He was a social critic with humanistic concerns. He depicted the individual in the context of society; his characters were always expressive of their social milieu. He did not moralize or judge, but simply focused attention on social realities. The influence of his inventions, theories and teaching is especially evident today in the newest movement in theatrical dance, the German *Tanztheater*.

Dance Drama, Modern Dance and *Tanztheater*

When Jooss was asked in an interview how he managed to make his dancers such good actors, he replied: "by never teaching them acting." He explained:

> The particular style of [*The Green*] *Table* is that acting and movement in itself are not separable; that acting is entirely dissolved into movement, [it] is cued to action so it is a strong amalgamation of action and pure movement which I think is the main feature of *Table*. (Terry, 1967)

This is in fact the key to all of Jooss's choreography: dramatic action is communicated through pure movement.

The merging of dramatic action with pure movement sounds paradoxical to some contemporary ears. Dramatic dance and abstract dance are often placed at opposite extremes of the continuum of theatrical dance. Dance drama has traditionally been associated with classical ballet, pure movement with contemporary dance. Until recently in Western dance history, those two dance forms have often been treated as competitive opposites. This has been an unfortunate error.

Dance as an art form has evolved dialectically, with periods of rebellion and rejection followed by consolidation of the new with the old. The obvious example of this is the rebellion of "modern dance" against classical ballet that dates from the 1920's. Sixty years later, Martha Graham declared that she "had no quarrel with classical ballet" and began using ballet stars as guest artists. Suddenly Graham company members began showing up in ballet classes. Overnight the turned-out feet and pointed toe stopped being anathema in modern dance. In "post modern" and "new wave" dance the two forms consolidated into unrestricted technical bravura or minimalistic conceptualism that cut across or dispensed with all techniques and vocabularies.

Jooss belonged to a tradition that has stressed the common properties of expression and communication which run through all expressive dance forms. Delsarte and Laban stand out as pioneers for having explored a universal psychology and mechanics of movement that can serve as the basis for communication in dance. Both maintained that all movement, the ordinary gesture as much as the stylized vocabulary of dance movement, originates in an inner attitude. This claim has shaped much of contemporary dance theater, even though its universal implications have often been ignored (Shawn, 1963, p.31).

Meaning and expression in dance should not be confused with a story line. Many works by modern dance choreographers carry great dramatic meaning while lacking any explicit plot. On the other hand, Jooss's dance dramas are expressive in ways that go beyond the telling of a story. They reveal the psychology and the motivation of the characters, establish mood and atmosphere, and reflect upon social and moral issues. The feature that fosters communication and is common to all expressive dance is what critic John Martin termed *metakinesis*:

> Movement, then, is a medium for the transference of an aesthetic and emotional concept from the consciousness of one individual to that of another. This should not be as strange an idea as it seems to be. Back as far as Plato, and perhaps farther, it has been toyed with by the metaphysical philosophers. Kinesis is the name they gave to physical movement, and in an obscure footnote in Webster's Dictionary — so common a source of reference as that! — we find that there is correlated with kinesis a supposed psychic accompaniment called metakinesis, this correlation growing from the theory that the physical and the psychical are merely two aspects of a single underlying reality. (Martin, 1965, p.13)

The single reality expressed through metakinesis is the emotion motivating the movement. The dancer communicates directly to his audience. Passions and sentiments which go beyond words are grasped in kinetic empathy. The French choreographer and dance reformer Jean George Noverre realized this when he wrote in 1760:

> Action in relation to dancing is the art of transferring our sentiments and passions to the souls of the spectators by means of the true expression of our movements, gestures and features. (Noverre, 1968, p.99)

These doctrines inspired the early modern dance pioneers to seek a radical departure from the strict and highly stylized classical technique in dance. They searched their bodies and their souls for points of departure, and found new ways of anchoring expressive dance in natural movement.

Mary Wigman believed that the dancer was propelled by the force of controlled inhalation and exhalation.[1] She explored and invented new, fresh movement to express the essence of a mood or an emotion (Howe, 1985, p.106). She believed that dance is "a living language" and that the source of its expression is "the living breath" which she called "the pulsebeat of the life of dance." This ordinary and indispensable act served the modern dancer as a link between the everyday motion of the body and dance movement. In Wigman's words:

> Movement gives meaning and significance to the artistically shaped and formed gesture language. For the dance becomes understandable only when it respects and preserves its meaning relative to the natural movement-language of man. (Wigman, 1966, p.10)

Similarly, for Martha Graham the power of expression lay in the contraction and release of the solar plexus, also a breath-related exercise. The quick and forceful expulsion of air by the diaphragm contracts the chest, which caves in as if from an invisible punch, pulling and contracting with it the entire torso and pelvic area. The movement is the physical equivalent of a psychic blow. The discovery and perfection of this movement cost Graham considerable effort:

> She would sit absolutely still, concentrating on the action of inhaling and exhaling. Inhaling gave her a sense of power, a feeling of the body renewing itself; exhaling was basically a letting go of the spirit as well as of the breath. But it wasn't passive. She tried to classify the movements muscularly by calling them "contraction" for the act of exhalation and "release" for the act of inhalation. But even the words had an emotional ring to them. And the movements of the body which coordinated with the breathing acts became more and more expressive as Martha built up the dimensions of the inhalation-exhalation rhythms. (Stodelle, 1984, p.48)

Both Wigman and Graham argued that the meaning of movement comes from expressing inner feelings and that the dancer communicates these through metakinesis directly to his audience. "It only demands that dance be a moment of passionate, completely disciplined action, that it communicate participation to the nerves, the skin, the structure of the spectator," wrote Graham in 1937 (Armitage, 1966, p.84). Wigman wrote that the audience should:

> . . . allow the rhythm, the music, the very movement of the dancer's body to stimulate the same feeling and emotional mood within itself, as this mood and emotional condition has stimulated the dancer. It is only then that the audience will feel a strong emotional kinship with the dancer and will live through the vital experiences behind the dance-creation. (Copeland, 1985, p.306)

The early modern dance choreographers strongly held that all meaningful dance movement originates in inner experience. "Movement without a motivation is unthinkable," said Doris Humphrey (Humphrey, 1959, p.110). She believed in the conscious motivation of dance movement by the choreographer that "communicates about people to people" (Humphrey, 1959, p.110). She founded her dance vocabulary on natural movement and considered the breath rhythm or breath flow to be one of its basic elements:

> In the dance we can use the simple rise and fall of the breath in its original location of the chest, but this is by no means all. The idea of breath rhythm − the inhalation, the suspension and the exhalation − can be transferred to other parts of the body. One can "breathe" with the knees, or the arms, or the whole body. (Humphrey, 1959, p.107)

In the 18th Century Noverre had pleaded for the use of pantomime as a dramatic element in ballets. By the 20th Century the conventional balletic pantomime had become rigidly stylized and devoid of emotion. Recognizing this, the great choreographer of Diaghilev's Ballets Russes, Michel Fokine, argued for a deeper unity of expression in which "the whole body of the dancer should portray character and feeling" (Cohen, 1974, p.102). Fokine considered classical technique to be meaningful only when each movement signalled something beyond the purely physical. In a 1919 article entitled "The New Ballet" he wrote:

> In order to restore dancing its soul we must abandon fixed signs and devise others based on the laws of natural expression . . . Certainly, an *arabesque* is sensible when it idealizes the sign, because it suggests the body's straining to soar upward, the whole body is expressive. If there be no expression, no sign, but merely a foot raised in the position termed *en arabesque*, it looks foolish. (In Cohen, 1974, p.103)

Another great dramatic choreographer was Antony Tudor. He began his training with Marie Rambert, an associate of Fokine's in the Ballets Russes under Diaghilev. Tudor freed the arms and the upper torso and gave them the expressive quality that Fokine had called for:

> Another failing of ballet technique is that it is concentrated in
> the dancing of the lower limbs, whereas the whole body should
> dance. The whole body to the smallest muscle should be expressive,
> but ballet schools concentrate on exercises for the feet. The arms
> are limited to a few movements and the hands to one fixed position.
> What variety would not be possible if the dancer renounced the
> mannerism of rounded arms. (In Cohen, 1974, p.107)

Tudor was a master of the psychological ballet in which characterization
and relationships were of ultimate importance. A quick touch of the hair,
the shrug of a shoulder or a stroke on the cheek were the kind of ordinary
gestures which became part of his choreography. Nevertheless, he left nothing
to improvisation. He insisted that his dancers follow the movement he created
exactly. "If I've given you a role and you do the movements for that role
exactly the way I tell you to do them, you will master that characterization,"
he said in an interview (Cohen, 1974, p.178).

Remembering the early days, Jooss remarked:

> When I was working with Laban in the early 1920's, we had no
> Mary Wigman, no Martha Graham to look to, but I remember
> Antony Tudor coming to me in 1933, when the company danced
> at the Savoy in London, and telling me how he has been encouraged
> to see what we were doing. (Koch, 1976, p.8)

What Tudor saw in 1933 was a fully matured style of dance theater. Upon
the intellectual groundwork laid by Rudolf von Laban, Jooss had forged
an amalgam of classical ballet and modern dance. The aesthetic expression
was based on the reciprocity of emotion and movement and on the parallel
between a person's character and his gestures. A. V. Coton wrote of the
new dance theater summarizing Jooss's own statements:

> The medium of dance is the living human body with the power
> to convey ideas inherent in its movements . . . . In the dramatic
> dance . . . these pure imaginings of movement are fused with the
> dramatic idea, and the fusion of the two elements creates a new
> entity, the dance drama, whose subject matter is the thought of
> the creator crystallized into active suffering human characters. Its
> medium and its language is the dance, sequences of movements
> which have been subjected to the process of composition, which
> have been purified and harmonised in regard to each other, and
> in their relation to the space and rhythm they create. (Coton, 1946,
> p.29)

Today's German *Tanztheater* is comprised of many dissonant elements.
Movement is intermingled with words, gigantic environments are created on
stage, everyday objects are used deliberately out of context as props. Ordinary
street clothes replace costumes, and cross dressing and nudity are frequent.
Fragmentation and repetition of scenes, of movement and of words are

common devices. These diverse components are the result of influences from many different fields, but their significance as dance movement comes directly from the tradition established by Laban and Jooss. In many respects the contemporary *Tanztheater* is the artistic inheritor of the Jooss legacy.

The direct link of the *Tanztheater* choreographers to Jooss is through the teaching traditions and training of the Folkwangschule. All three of the best known innovators of the German *Tanztheater*, Pina Bausch, Reinhild Hoffmann and Susanne Linke, received training at the school. Pina Bausch studied with Jooss, performed in his company and began choreographing in his Master Class. Reinhild Hoffmann and Susanne Linke were students there at a later date.[2]

There are a number of aesthetic elements in *Tanztheater* that can be traced to Jooss. His work is the source of such compositional devices as the cinematic sequence of multiple scenes, the gesture as the basis of characterization, and the stylized natural movement as the anchor for a character's milieu. Social criticism and a concern with contemporary issues also link today's *Tanztheater* to the legacy of Jooss.

Jooss as Playwright of Movement

An important part of Jooss's legacy is his approach to dance movement, an approach that is alive (though metamorphosed) in today's German *Tanztheater* and in the pedagogical traditions of the Folkwangschule. Unlike the American modern dance pioneers, Jooss never codified his teachings in the form of a "Jooss Technique." When criticized for this, Jooss replied:

> I am often reproached that the style we teach is not clearly
> identifiable. But we are not teaching a specific style; what we teach
> is the dancer's craft. Style is a result of choreographic intention
> and choice. (Markard & Markard, 1985, p.149)

Jooss called himself "a playwright of movement" (Koch, 1976, p.8). In his choreography he used movement to construct a drama, and the dramatic significance is the unifier of everything else. This dramatic basis is what weaves together the elements of plot, characterization, motivation and expression. Technique is always a means of expression, and expressive movement has meaning because of its contribution to the drama.

The general relationship between movement and motivation is well established in the theater. It has been called the "biomechanics of acting" because of the fact that "particular patterns of muscular activity elicit particular emotions" (Brockett, 1974, p.521). The reverse is just as true: particular emotions elicit corresponding patterns of physical activity. This same reciprocal connection is at the heart of the way movement communicates in dance. It explains why the expressiveness of dance movement goes far beyond the sign language of mime and provides a basis for direct communication through metakinesis and kinetic empathy.

Jooss's choreographic technique and vocabulary reflect a reciprocity between the psychological and the physical. He explained in an interview that in his studies he had been:

. . . trying to find the movements which certain emotions create, and again in which way those movements affect the onlooker . . . My teacher, Laban, called it Eukinetik. But Laban's object is to make his pupils develop the work, not to remain at the same place where they left him, which so many have done. (Jooss, 1933, p.454)

In his earliest work with Laban, Jooss had worked on a new dance vocabulary that grew out of "Laban's movement teachings and his choreographic space principles, combined with the discipline of traditional ballet" (Markard, 1982, p.19). With the assistance of Sigurd Leeder, he developed it further into a method for the training of dancers, a method now known as the Jooss-Leeder Method.[3] Much of Jooss's choreography is based on the same movement material.

The Jooss-Leeder Method is based on four principles: tension and relaxation; weight and strength; three basic rhythms; and the flow and guidance of movement. Just as in the case of the early modern dance choreographers, the elemental forces behind these principles are the pull of gravity and the flow of breath. Tension reflects the resistance to gravity, relaxation the assistance given to it. The cycle of exhalation and inhalation follows the pattern of tension and relaxation (Winerals, 1958, pp.17–19). A continuous flow of energy supplies the rhythmic force as it goes through initial, transitional, and terminal phases. The whole harmonious cycle can be seen as:

. . . the continuous flow of movement between the momentary suspension of activity at the peak of the wave and the momentary cessation of activity at the trough. In both moments tension and relaxation are balanced. (Winerals, 1958, p.25)

Tension is constantly flowing into relaxation and relaxation again becomes tension. The whole cycle is expressed in gathering or "scooping" movements and scattering or "strewing" motions. The initial, transitional and terminal rhythms represent a pendulum-like "swing" wherein the tension is gathered, the movement gains momentum, weight becomes strength and power, and the movement comes to a final climax immediately before the diminishing of energy begins.

Added to this central concept are the five basic ballet positions and the turnout of the feet, but not the pointe shoe. Jooss's dancers wear soft slippers or character shoes, according to the dramatic demands of their roles. Jooss explained that the pointe shoes "always got in the way as far as I was concerned. But I trained my dancers' feet so high that audiences often had the impression we were on pointe" (Koch, 1976, p.8).

Jooss uses this impression as a dramatic element in his dances. The Infanta in *Pavane*, in her final fright, rises on high half-toe: it exaggerates the tension of her precarious situation as the court begins its menacing advance. The Old Mother rises in a similar way as she walks haltingly toward Death. The lovers rise on tiptoe as they part, the Partisan pulls up when shot as if jerked upwards by the bullets, and the Young Girl becomes a puppet in the hands of the Profiteer as she exits walking stiffly on tiptoe. There is nothing arbitrary or formalistic about the rise on halfpointe in these instances: the posture and gesture are part of the dramatic expression. Gesture is not limited to the arms and the hands, but extends to the head, the legs and feet, or any part of the body.

Jooss regarded the body as an expressive whole. He attributed dramatic value to every movement, including the steps and positions of the classical ballet. An arabesque could express humility and romantic yearning, while the pirouette expressed physical vitality or abandonment in the whirl of the turn. A clear example of this is the Partisan's fast whirling solo as she abandons herself to her passionate desire for revenge. Jooss believed that if the choreographer understood the innate sense and meaning of each movement, he would use it only in a context that communicated an exact message, leaving mime superfluous. He said:

> Conformity is necessary also between the inner movement of the mind and the outer movement of the body . . . . Movement in the Jooss Ballets differs from the movement of the contemporary classical school mainly by its insistence on the correlation of body and mind. (Storey, 1943, p.456)

In the Jooss ballets the inner impulse controls the meaning of a movement, and there is meaning in each movement. At times the same movement can take on different emphasis and expressive value depending on its emotional context. For example, the lunge expresses the yearning to escape in the case of the Princess in *Pavane*. The tension of the movement flows outward and continues on into space through her arms and outward focused gaze. In the case of the Young Workingman of *Big City*, the lunge signifies disappointment, hopelessness. The arms are being restricted to the side of the body by the hands thrust into the pockets. The flow of energy is arrested, the gaze is level.

The flow of energy through the body regulates the movement's rhythm and changes the quality of action depending on the amount of freedom or control the body moves with. The flow depends on the amount of tension guiding and controlling the movement, and is connected with balance, coordination and the economy of movement. The movement flow of the body can be sequential in isolated movements, or synchronous when the body moves in a block. Movement flow gives the body its shape and design. Movement can be central or peripheral, curving or undeviating (Winerals, 1958, pp.40–41). The Profiteer moves in curving shapes and indirect circular paths in concentric movement patterns. Death moves on an undeviating path with weighty and angular movements, his posture straight. He gathers his strength, tensing his muscles, then releases the energy away from the center of the body sequentially in sweeping, slashing, thrusting movements.

The dynamic rhythms of the body are based on weight and strength. Strength is the inward concentration and outward expansion of tension as in the scattering, hurling movements of Death's solo. Weight and strength are connected, as are energy and strength. The more energy expended, the stronger the movement, as in Death's solo or the movements of the angry Mothers of *Big City* protecting their children from the Libertine. Light, soft movements are a consequence of peripheral release of energy, as in the movements of the young and innocent Infanta who seems to float like a feather (Winerals, 1958, p.90).

The position of the body in space has significance: the tilt of the Gentlemen in Black, or the square, erect posture of the Court in *Pavane*. When the Gentlemen in Black perform their see-saw tilts against the conference table, they create an image of argument: ideas and insults fly back and forth. The erect posture of the court shows rigidity and inflexibility. Death takes up a wide frontal stance, with arms spread to the sides, both powerful and threatening. The Mothers create a menacing outline with their wide stance and crossed arms. The fighting soldiers cut, slice and slash through space. Hurled horizontally, they land in crumpled falls, then roll to gather strength to spring up again.

The path of the body through surrounding space also has choreographic meaning. The circular paths of the Infanta, meandering within the linear path of her court, tell the whole story of her physical and emotional imprisonment. The diagonal path is the strongest straight path, as demonstrated by the powerful approach of the soldier shadowed by Death moving toward the Young Girl, or the procession of the dead crossing on the diagonal. The paths of the crowd in *Big City* create two entirely different images: the individualistic design of separate criss-crossing paths, then the well-ordered friendly display in which all cross the stage together, looking straight at the audience.

The facial expression follows the expression of the rest of the body; no special emphasis is placed on its significance or communicative powers. Jooss said:

> The important thing is for each muscle to be ready for participation in the action of each movement; to allow the face as well as the leg, or any part of the body for that matter, to assume the specific tension belonging to the expression of the present moment. Consequently I regard the dancer inadequate whose face does not participate equally with hands, legs and torso in the general expression of the body. He may as well hesitate to use his right arm whilst moving freely with the rest of his body. (Storey, 1943, p.455)

All the dramatic expression in the Jooss ballets is in the choreography. Based on the principles of Eukinetics and Choreutics, the choreography contains within itself the means to express every dramatic nuance the artist wishes to communicate. All decorative embellishments have been excluded because they are unnecessary. Jooss took elements from the discipline of classical ballet only when he found that they enhanced the expressiveness and dramatic power of his choreography. For example, he considered the conventional *pas de deux* formalistic and empty. Lifts that have no other purpose than to simulate flight or show the taut balletic line should be eliminated as extraneous to human drama (Jooss, 1933, p.453). Likewise with all virtuosic technical feats that show off the skills of individual dancers but add nothing to the dramatic content.

In Jooss's ballets every movement is governed by a motivating reason. There is nothing extraneous; the content shapes the form. When Jooss spoke of the future of dance he said:

> The future can only be dominated by an art whose main factors
> and elements of form constitute a language of movement. Please
> do not misunderstand my words. I do not mean a formal language
> where every movement has an understood meaning, like in some
> oriental dances. What I mean is that every movement would speak.
> The dance should be able to talk in a language of movement. The
> audience ought to be able to hear with their eyes. Very often it
> is possible to interpret in dancing something which can not be said
> with words. (Jooss, 1933, p.454)

Content shapes form. By maintaining this principle with unswerving integrity,
Jooss created the purest form of dance theater that the history of dance
has ever seen.

Jooss as Choreographer

The aesthetic elements of choreography are: the harmony and contrast of
visual design in space; the phrasing of the movement combinations and
transitions in time; the dynamics of movement execution with the muscular
force of energy; and the vocabulary, technique, and style which give shape,
line and texture to the movement. Costumes, props, lighting and staging
complete the choreography and make the dance into a finished theatrical
production.

The concept of choreographic design is related to form. Laban analyzed
design in terms of spatial directions: the shape of the body in space and
the path the body takes through space. Design includes the plasticity of the
body, three-dimensionality, the arrangements and groupings of dancers on
the stage, the use of symmetry and asymmetry, and the focus of attention
and direction. Spatial directions and the arrangements of the individual
dancers and groups of dancers on the stage are just as meaningful in the
Jooss ballets as are movement and gesture. There are no stars or "star-turns."
The protagonist gains his importance from the significance of his character,
the dancer from the significance of the character he plays in the drama.
All of the dancers who are on stage at any one point are necessary to the
drama and form an integral part of the action.

The clearest example of the significance of design in a Jooss ballet is
Pavane, where the direction of the movement, the floor patterns and the
grouping of the dancers delineate and frame the action. The linear design
of the court, with the dancers in two rows on the two sides of the stage,
defines the perimeters of the action. In order to avoid the tedium of symmetry,
Jooss placed three men on the one side and five women on the other.

Another example of design is the opening scene of *Big City*. As the
one-dimensional linear movement pattern across the stage switches to a three-
dimensional plastic movement and back again, the emphasis shifts from
anonymity to individuality. As a result, the scene takes on a cinematic quality.
At the same time the design creates a pattern of grids forming the imaginary
streets and avenues of a busy, bustling city. Other examples of contrasting

designs in space are the sharp, tense, angular and weighty movements and posture of Death and the curving, circular, sinuous lines of the Profiteer; or the strong eccentric spirals and lunges of the young Partisan and the bent, gravity-bound concentric movements of the Old Mother. In each case, design is a part of the choreographic meaning.

Choreographic phrasing is related to musical properties. According to George Balanchine, the choreographer, like the musician, frees himself from the constraints of everyday time and uses his technical skills to transform his experience and knowledge into dynamic design. He coordinates motion into a rhythmic flow in time, so that it becomes significant movement (Chujoy & Manchester, 1967, p.202). Jooss himself was superbly musical; as a young man he studied voice and piano at the Stuttgart Academy of Music. He took delight in matching complex musical phrasing with equally intricate choreographic phrases. An example of this is *Ball in Old Vienna*. Bengt Häger writes:

> For the dancers, *Ball in Old Vienna* is extremely demanding, and can be rendered only by very rhythmically and musically gifted artists, able to grasp the intricate variations and contrapuntally interwoven movements. (Häger, in press)

The relationship of movement to music in the Charleston and the musette of *Big City* is similarly complex and difficult. Here the rhythmic changes affect mood changes appropriate to the unfolding drama. In the movement of the court in *Pavane* and in Death's solo in *The Green Table*, the steps cut across the accompanying musical measure at a crucial moment, enhancing the dynamic force of the action.

The musical accompaniment of Jooss ballets consisted of two grand pianos. This practice was the practical idea of the composer F. A. Cohen, Jooss's longest and closest musical collaborator. When preparing for the 1932 Paris choreographic competition, Cohen realized that with the large number of companies participating, rehearsal time with the resident orchestra would be restricted. For this reason he suggested the use of two pianos. At the performance of *The Green Table*, two grand pianos were placed in the orchestra pit. This proved so successful in every way that it became a hallmark of the company (Häger, in press).

The artistic collaboration of Jooss and Cohen was an extraordinary partnership. Of the creation of *The Green Table*, Jooss said: "we worked like one person on it, we could never account for it" (Terry, 1967). Cohen believed that in compositions written for the dance, the musical form should emerge from the dramatic idea just as much as the choreographic form does. In this way the music and the dance would complement each other harmoniously.

Jooss choreographed on a human scale. It was not his purpose to defy gravity by leaps, jumps and lifts. Neither do his dancers spend much time working close to the floor. They move in the middle region, standing, walking, running, jumping, leaping or falling as the action requires, like actors in a silent play. This is why Jooss called himself "a playwright of movement." But in terms of Laban's "dynamosphere," which he called "the space in which our dynamic actions take place," Jooss's choreography moves in the accustomed range of human activity. Clear lines, sharp attacks and smooth transitions delineate the action. Choreography is a visual art: we perceive the dance by looking at it. Jean George Noverre wrote that a well composed ballet is ''a living picture of passions and manners which speaks to the soul through the eyes and touches upon the emotions'' (Noverre, 1968, p.16). Jooss greatly admired Noverre. While reflecting upon the use of traditional mime in classical ballet Jooss comments:

> If the great Noverre had been confronted with it, what thunderbolts he would have hurled at the heads of its miserable creators, at those deviating from the true, constantly evolving traditions inaugurated by him in his *Lettres sur la dance*, and to which every reformer up to and including Fokine has returned as the foundation of his reforms. I watch the present neglect of Noverre with ever growing concern, certain that at the present time his ''Letters'' ought to be the daily bread of every conscientious dancer who has real artistic ambitions. (Storey, 1943, p.456)

The aesthetics of Jooss's choreography, like that of Noverre, was based on reform, not on rebellion as with so many of the moderns. He consolidated the old and the new, the classical and the modern. At the Paris choreographic competition he gave the jury the following declaration which he called the ''credo'':[4]

> We believe in the Dance as an independent art of the Theater, an art which cannot be expressed in words, whose language is movement built up of forms resulting from emotions. We desire to serve the Dance of the Theater, which we look upon as the most intensely significant synthesis of living dramatic expression with the Dance properly so called. We aim therefore at discovering a choreography deriving equally from the contributions of modern art and from the technique of the classical ballet. We find the basis of our work in the whole range of human feeling and all phases of its infinite expression; and by concentrating on the ''essential'' we arrive at our form in the Dance.

Jooss looked for the significant movement, the gesture or motion which conveys the essence of a character, the core of his emotions and actions and the basis of his relationship to others and to society. He distilled each situation to its essence. Jooss's ballets are just as noteworthy for their compositional clarity and economy of expression as for their dramatic content. Each of the four Jooss ballets is constructed around a central theme with a beginning, development, climax and conclusion. Nothing extraneous distracts from the action. Critic John Martin wrote:

> The rapid panorama of the story is unfolded with such economy of means and such simplicity of intention that its eloquence is unanswerable . . . . In all his choreography Jooss shows his feeling for form and design and his easy and intelligent approach to music. (Martin, 1933)

Jooss strongly believed in a clear, theatrically legible dance form. He believed that some of the basic principles of the old classical forms should be adopted by the new dance to anchor the modern dance in technical discipline and give it the form it lacked. He said:

My objections to the two present forms of the dance are that the Classical Ballet ignores the emotions and remains simply outward forms, while the so-called Central European Dance has practically no outward form and only considers the emotions. (Jooss, 1933, p.453)

Jooss believed that in art we experience emotion through form, and that there are laws governing expression in every art form. His artistic goal was to give "adequate form to genuine human expression" (Storey, 1940, p.596). He achieved this goal not only through movement but also through the formal values of composition and the harmonious blend of all elements of stagecraft. The formal structure of Jooss's works consist of clarity; the development of a dominant theme and variations on this theme; the balance of various parts of the composition; variety and contrast, smooth transitions and the organic unity of the whole.

That all elements of a work should harmoniously complement each other corresponds to the idea of *Gesamtkunstwerk* or "total work of art," first conceived by Richard Wagner and later adopted by Gropius and the Bauhaus. The close collaboration of Jooss, Cohen and the designer Hein Heckroth contributes to this effect in the Jooss ballets. The costume designs, the few props and the lighting are necessary and critical parts of the drama. For example, the masks of the Gentlemen in Black contribute to the comic and at the same time foreboding character of the Prologue of *Green Table*. Death's ingenious makeup and costume are responsible for conveying the duality of his character and appearance as soldier and skeleton. The flag first stands for victory and hope, then becomes a symbol of defeat. A hat, a cape, a pair of gloves, each becomes a part of the action. A scene is made either pictorial or cinematic by the shades of lighting. In *Pavane* the dark red tones in the silk of the women's costume shimmer in the muted light like the fabrics in the painting of the old masters. The dance halls in *Big City* flatten out for a moment into cinematic one-dimensionality as the light changes between glitter and warmth. We can almost smell the cigarette smoke in the brothel of *The Green Table* as shafts of bright light cut through the dusky red and orange tones that splatter the floor and silhouette the dancers. A scene can change entirely through lighting effects, as when the crowd exits and a pale glow illuminates the Young Girl and the soldier in a barren place where Death approaches.

Jooss used no scenery. But his images are so powerful that battlefields, courtyards, palaces and brothels are conjured up on stage by the combined atmosphere of movement, music and drama. We see the hills where soldiers march and guerrillas kill, the back yard of the slums where children play, the cold marble palace from which the Infanta can't escape, the cabaret of the rich and the dance hall of the poor, and the brothel where refugee girls become prostitutes. When Allen Storey says that in the Jooss ballets "figures become units, soldiers become armies, brothels turn into nations," he is responding to Jooss's ability to give universal significance to his images (Storey, 1940, p.596).

Universality and symbolism were characteristic of expressionistic art. So were the use of generic characters or types, essentialism, the episodic or cinematic presentation of action, concerns with society, war and death, and the inspiration gained from primitive or Medieval Art (Howe, 1985, pp.96–97). These aesthetic elements of expressionism survived the demise of the movement itself and were perpetuated by the artists of the Neue Sachlichkeit or New Objectivity.

Jooss used those elements in his ballets, but he differs greatly from the expressionists. His quest is for structure and form; he lacks any desire to shock, to distort and to seek out the ugly. He is not interested in rebellion against established forms. In his fusion of the classical with the modern, his lack of mysticism, and his disinclination for political activism, he is far removed from the agenda of expressionism. Above all, Jooss did not accept self-expression and the purely subjective as art. Jooss was a realist for whom artistic form held supreme importance and essentialism meant perceptive and astute characterization and economy of expression. His concern with society and the individual was humanitarian. He was convinced that art would not change the political arrangements and that it should never be used as propaganda.

Where others assumed that spirituality leads away from the human realm, Jooss had a spiritual attitude toward human imagination itself. In a 1930 essay entitled *Tanzkunst* he wrote:[5]

> The spectator of such a dance has a perceptual experience of the communion of living men with the infinite. But the dancer who brings this communion into existence experiences the ultimate human happiness: to step beyond the petty wretchedness of everyday existence and to enter, body and soul, as a man of flesh and blood, into the heaven of all religions: the eternal creative imagination.

Jooss experienced this vision of eternity in his explorations of the down-to-earth, as he sought to deal objectively with the lives of real people and the problems of existing society.

Jooss as Social Commentator

In an essay entitled "The Importance of Ballets Jooss," critic Clive Barnes calls the Jooss ballets "socially significant dance allegories" (Barnes, 1953, p.10). He refers to them as "painfully moving, evocative, sincere and poetic" and judges *The Green Table* to be "one of the most significant works of ballet history."

Jooss always looked at the individual as part of a society, never as a separate entity. He was not interested in probing the dark secrets of the individual psyche. His characters were part of a milieu, and they came alive through their actions and reactions. Nor did Jooss pronounce judgments on social and moral issues as such. His method was to exhibit those issues as experienced by individuals in the society. He held up a mirror to society to show its imperfections, blemishes and deformities. He could be comical, gently mocking, tenderly lyrical or brutally honest, but he always showed genuine concern and involvement with humanity.

While identifying the major issues in the four ballets, it is useful to illustrate these themes in the larger corpus of Jooss ballets which survive only in scattered descriptions. In *Pavane* he dealt with the necessity of freedom and the effects of restrictions imposed upon the individual by an inflexible society. In *Big City* he explored class differences, the vulnerability of youth and the loneliness of the Metropolis. In *Ball in Old Vienna* he lightly touched upon the generation gap and the restrictions the old try to impose on the young. In *The Green Table* he focused on war and its consequences, the victimization of civilians (especially women) and the corruption bred by power and money.

The issue of war was a major concern of Jooss, as it was of most artists of the Weimar period. *The Green Table* contains his most concentrated statement on this issue, but he returned to it repeatedly in his work. In 1935, while already in exile, Jooss choreographed his first sequel to *The Green Table*. *The Mirror* deals with the ravages of war as experienced by its survivors: "the confusion and worries, the despair and the hopes of post-war mankind struggling to escape from the moral, social and political consequences of his own folly" (Coton, 1946, p.59). A large gambling table with a surface of painted squares was positioned center stage in one of the scenes, echoing *Green Table*. The scenario focused on the grim uncertainties of post-war civilian existence. The Man of Leisure, the Middle Class Man, and the Laborer have escaped the war together. Facing the problems of alienation, unemployment and crippling social inequities, they look for solutions in revolution, which creates even greater social chaos. Eventually the understanding and love of a fallen woman saves them.

Jooss believed that only an appeal to the noblest of human qualities, the possibility of redemption through understanding and unselfish love, held any hope of healing the wounds created by war. After his return to Essen he created *Journey in the Fog*, another memorial to human suffering in time of war. Here the focus was upon the fate of the refugee, the exile, and the prisoner of war.

In *Pavane* Jooss dealt with the inflexibility of society and the individual's need for freedom. A stylistic and thematic companion piece was *Ballade*, which also premiered in 1935. The program notes tell of a Queen who "sent a poisoned bouquet to the young Marquise, who had been too much favored by the King's attention" (Coton, 1946, p.53). Jooss choreographed variations on the court dance steps of the galliard and the passepied to indicate the formal behavior of the court. John Coleman composed accompanying variations on medieval French songs. The theme was the cruelty of court life and the ruthlessness of the absolute monarch.

In 1939 Jooss created *Chronica* to explore another aspect of the abuse of power. In the guise of a medieval Italian tale, he exposed the destructive nature of authoritarian rule and the misguidedness of the concept of a "benevolent" dictator (Coton, 1946, p.59).

The issue of authority in society leads on toward the problems of the European class structure. We have seen how *Big City* exposed the idle callousness of the rich, contrasting it with the honest morality of the working poor. In conjuring up the city as microcosm, Jooss showed his interest in the new social organizations and the changing value systems of the modern world.

The generation gap, treated lightly in *Ball in Old Vienna*, is given more serious treatment in *The Prodigal Son*, premiered in 1931 in Essen. There Jooss focussed upon the relationship between father and son. The sins of the son are committed against society. He is crowned King at the apex of his success and becomes an oppressor of his people. When he falls from favor he returns home repentantly to a forgiving father.

On the most universal level, Jooss was always preoccupied by the opposing forces of good and evil, the power of tolerance and love, and the need for understanding. In *Pandora*, choreographed in 1944, Jooss turned the mythological story of Pandora's box into an allegory on the warring forces of good and evil. Pandora is a beautiful but soulless young woman. When the Go-Getter opens her box (a gift from the gods) a multitude of monsters is released, among them the Machine God whom people begin to worship. Evil takes over. Only the innocent Youth who does not let go of the vision of Psyche can banish Pandora with her monsters and restore goodness to the world (Coton, 1946, p.66). In his interpretation of the piece, A. V. Coton writes:

> He can read in the work a penetrating because unforced comment on our eternal need of love: with "love" meant not as romantic allegory on sexuality, nor even particularly as that neighbourly good feeling which enables us to keep the peace happily, but meant as a willingness to tolerate and understand all men, stripping ourselves of prejudice and preconception, and accepting all human creation as part of ourselves, to know with our hearts as well as with our minds. (Coton, 1946, p.69)

We know in retrospect that the Weimar Republic was one of the most remarkable periods in modern civilization. It was a time of intellectual and artistic innovation unprecedented in modern history. The social and humanitarian issues explored by Jooss were a concern of most major artists of the period. As John Willett points out, too much emphasis has been placed on distortion and decadence as the hallmarks of Expressionism. To arrive at a balanced view, more emphasis must be given to the parallel movement known as the New Objectivity:

> A particular constructive vision originating at the end of the First World War, a new realism that sought methods of dealing both with real subjects and with real human needs, a sharply critical view of existing society and individuals and a determination to master new media and discover new collective approaches to the communication of artistic concepts. (Willett, 1978, p.11)

In dance it was Jooss who championed this critical but constructive new objective vision of society and of the individual with exceptional clarity.

Jooss in Historical Perspective

The roots of modern dance in Germany were physical culture, the theories of Emile Jaques Dalcroze and Rudolf von Laban, and the revolutionary concepts of Isadora Duncan. Their common starting-point lay in an attempt to free the body from constraints which had been imposed by society, and in the belief that a new spiritual man would emerge from an unrestricted body that learned to move with freedom and spontaneity. These beliefs led to the rebelliousness and stubbornly individualistic traits of the new dance in Germany. The Modern Dance — offspring of a thousand tendencies, impulses and desires — already existed. It fell to Jooss to elevate it from a series of manifestations, each centered on an individual or a pair of performers, into a method with shape, definition, laws and a pedagogy (Coton, 1946, p.71).

Jooss did not rebel; he was a consolidator. Out of the many existing trends, vocabularies, styles and techniques he chose what he considered appropriate for his own purposes and invented the rest. The result was a distinct form of theatrical dance. Subsequently, dance in Germany took three distinct routes of development: The Opera Ballet, *Ausdruckstanz*, and *Tanztheater*. In order to understand the distinctive nature of Jooss's invention, it is useful to compare his dance theater with the directions taken by those first two movements, the German embodiments of classical ballet and modern dance.

Jooss worked on the dramatic scale of classical ballet with the modest means of the modern dancer. His methods of presentation were akin to theatrical productions and lacked the grandiosity of the European "opera ballet." His productions were intimate; his company was always small, consisting of dancers he trained himself. He did not create spectacles, he created human drama. His characters were not supernatural, otherworldly or archaic creatures, but everyday people: old mothers, prostitutes, soldiers, refugees. Everyone on stage was a part of the drama: Jooss did not employ a decorative corps de ballet to fill gaps in the action. Male and female dancers held equal importance: the men did not lift and carry the women in the accustomed classical *pas de deux*. The principals performed no solo turns to show off technique. Clive Barnes wrote:

> The dancers are beautifully trained. As soloists they are capable
> of great expressiveness, as members of an ensemble they can
> suppress their individuality so completely that the ensemble looks
> as though it is directed by one mind, its movements being extensions
> of one body. (Barnes, 1953, p.10)

In the lack of scenery and the practical (even utilitarian) nature of costumes and design, the Jooss productions were drastically different from classical ballet with its lavish operatic decor, tutus and toeshoes. As we have seen, the only elements of the classical technique that Jooss adopted were the ones that made the body expressive, enhanced the discipline of training, and contributed to the dramatic expression of the choreography. Jooss said:

> My opinion is that the future belongs to the dramatic dance. This
> dance must combine all the elements of the abstract dance, not

only in the form of pantomime, but in the form of absolute dance. Just in the same way as the musical dramas of Wagner have revolutionized opera in their day, I see in this new dance a new theatrical art − a dumb theatre. This should be able to give expression to matters which the spoken stage cannot do. (Jooss, 1933, p.455)

American modern dance strove to achieve similar goals, but it focused less on dance theater and more on a form of absolute dance derived from natural movement. It is virtually impossible to speak of "modern dance" as a single phenomenon since it was influenced by so many individuals and factions, and took just as many divergent routes.

In Jooss's choreography, no one phenomenon is singled out as uniquely appropriate for expressing emotion, in the way that modern dance stresses contraction and release or fall and recovery. There is no emphasis on bare feet, natural movement, or being close to nature. Jooss was an urban choreographer with a strong interest in the social and moral issues of his time. He did not deliberately set out to discover new ways of moving, as each of the early modern dancers did. Movement for him was a means of delineating character and feeling, a way of communicating ideas and events to create a story. Technique was the dancer's craft, the repertoire of skills that must be mastered in order to communicate. Jooss explained his method of working:

The most difficult and most important matter is the artistic education of the dancer . . . . In my productions the roles are only partly written, and I mostly only sketch them out before rehearsals commence. I indicate to the artist what I wish him to convey to the audience and allow him to improvise and give form to his own emotions, and then I try to arrange my work on the lines I set out to do, but giving him as much of his own as possible. This I can only do with dancers from my own school; those who join me from the outside have first to be shown every step and gesture till they have participated in this intellectual and spiritual training. (Jooss, 1933, p.454)

The explanation for the successful fusion of ballet and modern dance in Jooss's work lies in his selectivity in choosing elements from each. The result was a curious combination of the discipline and structure of classical ballet with the freedom and fluidity of modern dance. The dramatic production provided the framework within which the characterizations were Jooss's greatest achievement. He created prototypes of the average man and woman, and archetypes of larger-than-life figures.

Jooss had great respect for the craft of the theater. He strove for theatrical legibility, maintained high standards of professionalism, and felt responsible to his audience. Weary of theatrical dilettantism, he felt that the serious work of the theater was to entertain. As a result his productions were carefully crafted from all points of view. Jooss used all of his talents in acting, music, photography, even ballroom dancing to gain a new perspective on the dance stage. Critic J. D. Lewitan called Jooss's works "minimal, systematic, cinematic, balletomodern" (Jackson, 1985, p.48).

Jooss was a key figure not only of German dance but of the new dance theater. Anna Kisselgoff wrote:

> He is more than the choreographer of *The Green Table* for which
> he is best known . . . . His principles are alive enough to constitute
> a heritage still valid for young choreographers to draw upon.
> (Kisselgoff, 1982, p.17)

In his opening address to the Second German Dance Congress which he organized in 1928 in Essen, Jooss declared that the way forward in dance involved a reconciliation of the achievements of modern dance with the tradition of the classical ballet (Markard & Markard, 1985, p.39). His statement was correct as a prediction that was fifty years ahead of its time. It took nearly that long for Martha Graham to admit that she had no quarrel with ballet and to invite classical dancers Rudolf Nureyev and Mikhail Baryishnikov as guest artists to perform with her company.

In recent years the New York City Ballet has performed works by modern dance choreographer Paul Taylor, and post-modern choreographer Twyla Tharp has held an official position with American Ballet Theater. The dichotomy between ballet and modern dance has been breached in vocabulary and technique at a hundred points. Most dancers receive training in more than one technique. Partly because of the flexibility of today's dancer and partly because ballet companies possess the resources that assure careful coaching and adequate rehearsal time, the four Jooss ballets are mainly performed by classical ballet companies today.

Jooss did much more than anticipate the trend of the future; he contributed very substantially to bringing it about. Upon his return to Essen in 1949, he plunged into the task of providing young dancers with training that was as rigorous as ballet, yet receptive to technical innovations from any quarter. At the time in Germany:

> For young dancers seeking an alternative to ballet, Essen offered
> the only opportunity for formalized training. The Folkwang School
> stands as probably the single most important source for
> development of postwar *Tanztheater*. (Manning, 1985, p.16)

The nearest thing to a spiritual heir to the Jooss tradition today is the high priestess of West Germany's contemporary *Tanztheater*, Pina Bausch. She is a former pupil of Jooss who also performed in his ballets. One of her roles was the Old Mother in *The Green Table*. Her sensitivity and feeling for form shine through the still photographs taken of her in the role. Pina Bausch graduated from the Folkwang School and spent six years with Jooss in intensive training in the Folkwang Dance Studio. She also spent two years studying at the Juilliard School in New York City.

Between her generation and Jooss's stands World War II and the experience of Hitler's Third Reich. The differences between her concept of dance theater and Jooss's are great. Roland Langer summed up the origin and current concept of *Tanztheater* in a *Dance Magazine* article:

New beginning came first in the 1960's. The most important
indigenous impulse came from German dance doyen Kurt Jooss
(1901–1979) at the Folkwang School in Essen. One of Jooss's most
eminent pupils was Pina Bausch who, together with her Wuppertal
Dance Theater, has evolved the concept *Tanztheater* (dance-
theater). A product of the 1970's, Tanztheater quickly became a
trademark of German modern dance throughout the world. The
name "Tanztheater" refers to a performance form that combines
dance, speaking, singing and chanting, conventional theater and
the use of props, set and costumes in one amalgam. It is performed
by trained dancers. Usually there is no narrative plot; instead,
specific situations, fears, and human conflicts are presented.
Audiences are stimulated to follow a train of thought or to reflect
on what the Tanztheater pieces *express*. It has been described as
a new twist on an old form: German Expressionism. (Langer, 1984,
p.46)

Bausch's works are a combination of the sixties "happenings" and early
expressionism, focused on the grotesque and the shocking. Her pieces are
expensively if not glamorously appointed spectacles made of intimate emotions
where dancers cavort in a field of carnations, or two feet of water, or tons
of dirt, all laboriously transported and dumped on stage. Jooss's influence
on her work is most evident in the interludes of tightly structured brilliant
movement phrases, in an evident concern with contemporary social issues,
and in the measure of realism which she brings to the dance stage (Servos,
1982, p.57).

Bausch is not the only influential dancer on the current German dance
scene who was influenced by Jooss. Reinhild Hoffmann and Susanne Linke
were both students of the Folkwang School, and both have made major
contributions to the new German *Tanztheater*. Among the non-German figures
who drew major inspiration from Jooss are the Swedish dancer-choreographer
Birgit Cullberg, who studied at the Jooss-Leeder School in England during
the 1930's and later became co-director of the Swedish Dance Theater, and
the American Lucas Hoving, who studied at Dartington Hall and danced
with the Ballets Jooss before joining the José Limon Dance Company.

Jooss himself made major contributions to the reconstruction of his
works from the early 1930's. Of *A Ball in Old Vienna* he remembered:

I had filmed the whole thing in 1932 with one of the first Kodak
movie cameras and promptly forgot about it in the confusion of
leaving Germany the following year. By sheer good luck the
complete record was preserved, and I was able to piece it together
and put it into notational form. (Koch, 1976, p.8)

In 1973 the Dance Notation Bureau in New York City officially undertook
to notate the four ballets of the *Ballets Jooss '32* program, and in 1976
the Joffrey Ballet revived the entire program with personal coaching by Jooss
and his daughter Anna Markard. Reporting on a contemporary interview
with Jooss in Germany, Roy Koch wrote:

When the Joffrey presents *The Big City, Pavane on the Death of an Infanta, A Ball in Old Vienna* and *The Green Table*, the evening will represent the total dance legacy of a career that has spanned more than half a century and had a profound influence on the course of modern dance. "These four ballets are all preserved in Laban notation exactly as they were first conceived, but none of my other ballets can be done now because they were never recorded," says Jooss. "In a way, though, I'm quite content for my work to be represented by these four – they are quite enough." (Koch, 1976, p.8)

Jooss was a modest man. The rest of us can hardly be content with the loss of so much of his choreography. Yet, Jooss was quite correct: those four ballets are quite enough to guarantee his immortality.

Notes

1. The elemental act of breathing as motivation for movement is a common thread which runs through the technical basis of modern dance choreography. Alma Hawkins writes:
    No doubt the aliveness of movement is related to breathing. The feeling center we have been discussing is also the location and the mechanism that controls breathing, and the cycle of inhalation and exhalation is the very essence of life. The dancer, very much aware of moving in relation to breathing, knows that each movement must be filled with breath if it is to be "alive." The layman would think it very strange to talk about filling the arms and legs with breath, but not so the dancer. (Hawkins, 1964, p.80)
2. Susanne Linke also studied personally with Mary Wigman, to whom she attributes a charismatic and nearly mystical transmission of the essence of her art. Linke conveyed these thoughts in obscure remarks made informally at the Society of Dance History Scholars Conference in New York City in January 1986.
3. Jean Cebron, teacher of the Jooss-Leeder Method at the Folkwangschule and a former member of Ballets Jooss, is one of the foremost exponents of this technique. His teaching and coaching take him all over the world, and when in New York he gives master classes for the José Limon Company. The Humphrey-Limon technique has many elements in common with the Jooss-Leeder method, most significantly the concepts of balance and unbalance, tension and relaxation. Mr. Cebron credits Lucas Hoving, a member of Ballets Jooss who later joined the Limon company, with bringing the insights of Jooss to the Humphrey-Limon technique (personal communication with Jean Cebron, April 1985). Critic Jack Anderson has reported that the Director of the Limon Company "considers the Limon and the Jooss-Leeder approaches thoroughly compatible" (Anderson, 1986b).
4. Manuscript in the Elsa Kahl Cohen archives.
5. Manuscript in the Elsa Kahl Cohen archives. The original text is in German.

APPENDIX: THE JOOSS BALLETS

When titles are given in two languages, the original title is listed first, but the alphabetical ordering is determined by the English title.

Acis und Galathea
    Music: Georg Friedrich Händel
    Design: Veniero Colosanti/John Moore
    Date: 1972
    Place: Salzburg Festspiele, Germany
    Under the Direction of: Herbert Graf

Der Nachmittag eines Fauns/Afternoon of a Faun
    Music: Claude Debussy
    Design: Hermann Markard
    Date: March 8, 1965
    Place: Leverkusen
    Company: Folkwangballett

Le Bal
    Music: Vittorio Rieti
    Design: Hein Heckroth
    Date: November 1930
    Place: Opera House, Essen, Germany
    Company: Folkwang Tanzbühne Essen

A Ball in Old Vienna/Ein Ball in Alt-Wien
    Libretto: Kurt Jooss
    Music: Joseph Lanner (arranged by Fritz A. Cohen)
    Design: Aino Siimola
    Date: November 21, 1932
    Place: Opera House, Köln, Germany
    Company: Folkwang Tanzbühne, Essen, Germany

Ballade
    Libretto: Kurt Jooss
    Music: John Coleman
    Design: Hein Heckroth
    Date: September 23, 1935
    Place: Opera House, Manchester, England
    Company: Ballets Jooss

Belsazar
    Music: Georg Friedrich Händel
    Design: Veniero Colosanti/John Moore
    Date: March 1972
    Place: Grand Theatre, Geneva, Switzerland
    Under the Direction of: Herbert Graf

Grosstadt von Heute/Big City
    Libretto: Kurt Jooss
    Music: Alexandre Tansman
    Design: Hein Heckroth
    Date: November 21, 1932
    Place: Opera House, Köln, Germany
    Company: Folkwang Tanzbühne Essen

Big City/Grosstadt
    Libretto: Kurt Jooss
    Music: Alexandre Tansman
    Design: Hein Heckroth
    Date: 1935
    Place: Dartington Hall, Dartington, England
    Company: Ballets Jooss

Castor und Pollux
    Music: Jean-Philippe Rameau
    Design: Jean-Pierre Ponnelle
    Date: 1962
    Place: Schwetzinger Festspiele, Opera House, Essen, Germany
    Under the Direction of: Erich Schumacher

Catulli Carmina
    Music: Carl Orff
    Design: Dominik Hartmann
    Date: October 22, 1956
    Place: Opera House, Düsseldorf, Germany

Chronica
    Libretto: Kurt Jooss
    Music: Berthold Goldschmidt
    Design: Dimitri Bouchène
    Date: February 14, 1939
    Place: Arts Theatre, Cambridge, England
    Company: Ballets Jooss

Colombinade
    Libretto: Kurt Jooss
    Music: Johann Strauss/Aleida Montijn
    Design: Rochus Gliese
    Date: 1951
    Place: Opera House, Essen, Germany
    Company: Folkwang Tanztheater/Ballets Jooss

Company at the Manor
    Libretto: Kurt Jooss
    Music: Ludwig van Beethoven
    Design: Doris Zinkeisen
    Date: February 15, 1943
    Place: Arts Theatre, Cambridge, England
    Company: Ballets Jooss

Coppelia
    Music: Leo Delibes
    Design: Hein Heckroth
    Date: February 25, 1931
    Place: Opera House, Essen, Germany
    Company: Folkwang Tanzbühne Essen

Der Dämon
    Music: Paul Hindemith
    Design: Hein Heckroth
    Date: March 1925
    Place: Municipal Theater, Münster, Germany
    Company: Neue Tanzbühne

Dido und Aeneas/Epilog
    Libretto: Kurt Jooss
    Music: Henry Purcell
    Design: Ekkehard Grubler
    Date: 1966
    Place: Schwetzinger Festspiele, Opera House, Essen, Germany
    Under the Direction of: Erich Schumacher

Dithyrambus
    Libretto: Kurt Jooss
    Music: Georg Friedrich Händel
    Design: Dimitri Bouchène
    Date: 1951
    Place: Opera House, Essen, Germany
    Company: Folkwang Tanztheater/Ballett Jooss

Drosselbart
    Libretto: Kurt Jooss
    Music: Wolfgang Amadeus Mozart
    Design: Hein Heckroth
    Date: March 1929
    Place: Opera House, Essen, Germany
    Company: Folkwang-Tanztheater-Studio

Die Feenkönigin/The Fairy Queen
    Music: Henry Purcell
    Design: Jean-Pierre Ponelle
    Date: 1959
    Place: Schwetzinger Festspiele, Opera House, Essen, Germany
    Under the Direction of: Erich Schumacher

Gaukelei
    Music: Fritz A. Cohen
    Design: Hermann Haerdtlein
    Date: May 2, 1930
    Place: Opera House, Essen, Germany
    Company: Folkwang-Tanztheater-Studio

Die Geschichte vom Soldaten
    Music: Igor Stravinsky
    Design: Hein Heckroth
    Date: 1931
    Place: Opera House, Essen, Germany
    Company: Folkwang Tanzbühne Essen

Der Grüne Tisch/The Green Table
    Libretto: Kurt Jooss
    Music: Fritz A. Cohen
    Design: Hein Heckroth
    Date: July 3, 1932
    Place: Théatre des Champs-Élysées, Paris, France
    Company: Folkwang Tanzbühne Essen

Groteske
    Libretto: Kurt Jooss
    Design: Hein Heckroth
    Date: 1925
    Place: Municipal Theater, Münster, Germany
    Company: Neue Tanzbühne

Johann Strauss, Tonight!
    Libretto: Kurt Jooss
    Music: Johann Strauss (arranged by Fritz A. Cohen)
    Design: Georg Krista
    Date: October 21, 1935
    Place: Gaiety Theatre, London, England
    Company: Ballets Jooss

Weg im Nebel/Journey in the Fog 1952
    Libretto: Kurt Jooss
    Music: Aleida Montijn
    Design: Robert Pudlich
    Date: 1952
    Place: Opera House, Essen, Germany
    Company: Folkwang Tanztheater/Ballets Jooss

Juventud
    Libretto: Kurt Jooss
    Music: Georg Friedrich Händel
    Design: Dimitri Bouchène
    Date: 1948
    Place: Santiago de Chile
    Company: Ballet del Instituto Musical

Kaschemme
    Libretto: Kurt Jooss
    Music: Fritz A. Cohen
    Design: Hein Heckroth
    Date: October 1926
    Place: Municipal Theatre, Münster, Germany
    Company: Neue Tanzbühne

The Mirror/Der Spiegel
    Libretto: Kurt Jooss
    Music: Fritz A. Cohen
    Design: Hein Heckroth
    Date: September 28, 1935
    Place: Opera House, Manchester, England
    Company: Ballets Jooss

Nachtzug/Night Train
    Music: Alexandre Tansman
    Design: Robert Pudlich
    Date: 1952
    Place: Opera House, Essen, Germany
    Company: Folkwang Tanztheater/Ballets Jooss

Pandora
    Libretto: Kurt Jooss
    Music: Roberto Gerhard
    Design: Hein Heckroth
    Date: January 26, 1944
    Place: Arts Theatre, Cambridge, England
    Company: Ballets Jooss

Pavane auf den Tod einer Infantin/Pavane on the Death of an Infanta
   Libretto: Kurt Jooss
   Music: Maurice Ravel
   Design: Sigurd Leeder
   Date: October 1929
   Place: Folkwang Museum, Essen, Germany
   Company: Folkwang-Tanztheater-Studio

Persephone
   Music: Igor Stravinsky
   Design: Andre Barsacq
   Date: April 30, 1934
   Place: Paris Opera, Paris, France
   Company: Ida Rubinstein

Persephone
   Music: Igor Stravinsky
   Design: Dominik Hartmann
   Date: April 16, 1955
   Place: Opera House, Düsseldorf, Germany

Persephone
   Music: Igor Stravinsky
   Design: Hein Heckroth
   Date: March 8, 1964
   Place: Opera House, Essen, Germany

Persisches Ballett
   Music: Egon Wellesz
   Design: Hein Heckroth
   Date: July, 1924
   Place: Donaueschinger Musiktäge, Germany
   Company: Neue Tanzbühne

Petrouchka
   Music: Igor Stravinsky
   Design: Hein Heckroth
   Date: February, 1930
   Place: Opera House, Essen, Germany
   Company: Folkwang-Tanztheater-Studio

Phasen/Phases
   Libretto: Kurt Jooss
   Music: Erich Sehlbach
   Design: Hermann Markard
   Date: 1966
   Place: Stadthalle Mülheim, Germany
   Company: Folkwangballett

Polovetzer Tanze
    Music: Alexander Borodin
    Design: Hein Heckroth
    Date: November 1930
    Place: Opera House, Essen, Germany
    Company: Folkwang Tanzbühne Essen

Der verlorene Sohn/The Prodigal Son
    Music: Prokofiev
    Design: Hein Heckroth
    Date: May 28, 1931
    Place: Opera House, Essen, Germany
    Company: Folkwang Tanzbühne Essen

The Prodigal Son/Der verlorene Sohn
    Libretto: Kurt Jooss
    Music: Fritz A. Cohen
    Design: Hein Heckroth
    Date: October 6, 1933
    Place: Stadschouwburg, Amsterdam, Holland
    Company: Ballets Jooss

The Prodigal Son/Der verlorene Sohn
    Libretto: Kurt Jooss
    Music: Fritz A. Cohen
    Design: Dimitri Bouchène
    Date: October 1939
    Place: Prince's Theatre, Bristol, England
    Company: Ballets Jooss

Der verlorene Sohn/The Prodigal Son
    Libretto: Kurt Jooss
    Music: Fritz A. Cohen
    Design: Dominik Hartmann
    Date: May 23, 1956
    Place: Opera House, Düsseldorf, Germany

Pulcinella
    Music: Igor Stravinsky
    Design: Hein Heckroth
    Date: April, 1932
    Place: Opera House, Essen, Germany
    Company: Folkwang Tanzbühne Essen

Rappresentazione di anima e di corpo
    Music: Emilio del Cavalieri
    Design: Veniero Colosanti/John Moore
    Date: 1968
    Place: Salzburger Festspiele
    Under the Direction of: Herbert Graf

Seltsames Septett
    Libretto: Kurt Jooss
    Design: Sigurd Leeder
    Date: 1928
    Place: Opera House, Essen, Germany
    Company: Folkwang-Tanztheater-Studio

Seven Heroes/Die sieben Schwaben
    Libretto: Kurt Jooss
    Music: Henry Purcell (arranged by Fritz A. Cohen)
    Date: October 1, 1933
    Place: Schouwburg Maastricht, Holland
    Company: Ballets Jooss

Seven Heroes/Die sieben Schwaben
    Libretto: Kurt Jooss
    Music: Henry Purcell (arranged by Fritz A. Cohen)
    Design: Hein Heckroth
    Date: October 9, 1937
    Place: Lyric Theatre, Baltimore, USA
    Company: Ballets Jooss

Die Brautfahrt/A Spring Tale
    Libretto: Kurt Jooss
    Music: Jean-Philippe Rameau/Francois Couperin
    Design: Hein Heckroth
    Date: May 1925
    Place: Municipal Theater, Münster, Germany
    Company: Neue Tanzbühne

A Spring Tale/Die Brautfahrt
    Libretto: Kurt Jooss
    Music: Fritz A. Cohen
    Design: Hein Heckroth
    Date: February 8, 1939
    Place: New Theatre, Oxford, England
    Company: Ballets Jooss

Suite 1929
    Libretto: Kurt Jooss
    Music: Fritz A. Cohen
    Design: Hein Heckroth
    Date: October 1929
    Place: Opera House, Essen, Germany
    Company: Folkwang-Tanztheater-Studio

Tanz-Suite
    Libretto: Kurt Jooss
    Music: Ernst Toch
    Design: Hein Heckroth
    Date: 1924
    Place: Municipal Theatre, Münster, Germany
    Company: Neue Tanzbühne

Tragödie
    Libretto: Kurt Jooss
    Music: Fritz A. Cohen
    Design: Hein Heckroth
    Date: May 1926
    Place: Municipal Theater, Münster, Germany
    Company: Neue Tanzbühne

Zimmer Nr. 13
    Libretto: Kurt Jooss
    Music: Fritz A. Cohen
    Design: Hein Heckroth
    Date: October 1929
    Place: Opera House, Essen, Germany
    Company: Folkwang-Tanztheater-Studio

BIBLIOGRAPHY

Adler, N. (1984) Reconstructing the dances of Isadora Duncan. *Drama Review*, 28(3).

Acocella, J. and Garafola, L. (1991) (Eds.) *André Levinson on dance writings from Paris in the twenties*. Hanover: Wesleyan University Press.

— (1988a) European angst vs. American cool: continental divide. *7 Days*, April 13, pp. 45–46.

— (1988b) Pina Bausch Tanztheater Wuppertal. *7 Days*, July 20, pp. 46–47.

Allen, R.F. (1983) *Literary life in German Expressionism and the Berlin circles*. Ann Arbor, Michigan: UMI Research Press.

Amberg G. (1949) *Ballet: the emergence of an American art*. New York: Mentor Books.

Anderson, J. (1986a) *Ballet and modern dance, a concise history*. Princeton: Princeton Book Company.

— (1986b) German dance finds a home in the Limon Company. *The New York Times*, February 23, section 2, p.8.

Arbeau, T. (1969) *Orchesography* (C. Beaumont, trans.). New York: Dover Publications. (Originally published, 1588).

Armitage, G. (1966) *Martha Graham*. New York: Dance Horizons. (Originally published, 1937).

Au, S. (1988) *Ballet and modern dance*. London: Thames and Hudson.

— (1979) A man of movement: Rudolf Laban, 1879–1958. *Dance Magazine*, June, pp.102–105.

Balanchine, G. (1967) Notes on choreography. In A. Chujoy & P.W. Manchester (Eds.), *The Dance Encyclopedia*. New York: Simon and Schuster.

Barnes, C. (1967) The Green Table, Jooss's durable 1932 ballet is performed by Joffrey Company at City Center. *The New York Times*, March 10.

— (1953) The importance of Ballets Jooss. *Dance and Dancers*, June, p.10.

Barry, H. (1983) *German Expressionists, Die Brücke and Der Blaue Reiter*. London: Jupiter Books.

Bartenieff, I. and Hutchinson, A. (1949) A tribute to Rudolf Laban. *Dance Observer*, December, pp.145–146.

Bell-Kanner, K. (1991) *The life and times of Ellen von Frankenberg*. London: Harwood Academic Publishers.

Benson, R. (1984) *German Expressionist drama: Ernst Toller and Georg Kaiser*. New York: Grove Press.

Bentley, E. (1981) *The Brecht commentaries: 1943–1980*. New York: Grove Press.

Best, D. (1974) *Expression in movement and the arts: A philosophical inquiry*. Edinburgh: Lepus Books.

Blance, A. (1982) *Weimar Germany: writers and politics*. Edinburgh: Scottish Academic Press.

Blair, F. (1986) *Isadora*. New York: McGraw-Hill.

Bloch, E. (1990) *Heritage of our times*. Los Angeles: University of California Press.

Brockett, O.G. (1974) *History of the theatre* (2nd ed.). Boston: Allyn and Bacon. (Originally published, 1968).

Buckle, R. (1980) *Buckle at the ballet: selected dance criticism*. New York: Atheneum.

— (1971) *Nijinsky*. New York: Simon and Schuster.

Clarke, M. (1946) Ballets Jooss. *Dance Magazine*, February.

Cohen, S.J. (1963) Antony Tudor: the years in America. *Dance Perspectives 18*.

— (1974) *Dance as a theater art*. New York: Dodd Mead & Co.

— (1972) *Next week Swan Lake: reflections on dance and dances*. Middletown, Connecticut: Wesleyan University Press.

— (1962) A prolegomenon to an aesthetics of dance. *Journal of Aesthetics and Art Criticism*, 21(1), 19–26.

Coton, A.V. (1946) *The New Ballet: Kurt Jooss and his work*. London: Dennis Dobson.
— (1953) Return of Ballets Jooss. *The Dancing Times*, April.
— (1975) *Writings on dance 1938–1968*. London: Dance Books.
Croce, A. (1977) *Afterimages*. New York: Alfred A. Knopf.
— (1982) *Going to the dance*. New York: Alfred A. Knopf.
Curtin, J. (1985) Reconstructing a 20's ballet. *The New York Times*, September 29.
Dalcroze, E.J. (1928) *Rhythm, music, and education*. New York, Putnam's Sons.
De Moroda, D. (1935) A day with Kurt Jooss. *The Dancing Times*, May, pp.140–142.
Denby, E. (1968) *Looking at the dance*. New York: Horizon Press.
Dewey, J. (1958) *Art as experience*. New York: G.P. Putnam's Sons. (Originally published, 1934).
Dufrenne, M. (1973) *The phenomenology of aesthetic experience* (E.S. Casey, trans.). Evanston: Northwestern University Press.
Dukes, A. (1939) Ballet 1939: the scene in Europe. *Theater Arts*, September.
Dunning, J. (1986) Paying tribute to a patriarch of modern dance. *The New York Times*, February 28, p.26.
Ekstein, M. (1989) *Rites of Spring: The great war and the birth of the modern age*, New York: Bantam Press.
Friedrich, O. (1972) *Before the deluge: a portrait of Berlin in the 1920's*. New York: Harper and Row.
Garraty, J.A. & Gay, P. (1972) (Eds.). *The Columbia history of the world*. New York: Harper and Row.
Gay, P. (1974) *Weimar culture: the outsider as insider*. Middlesex, England: Penguin Books. (Originally published, 1969).
Girouard, M. (1985) *Cities and people: a social and architectural history*. New Haven: Yale University Press.
Gowing, L. (1936) Notes on the Ballets Jooss. *The Dancing Times*, November.
Grant, G. (1969) *Technical manual and dictionary of classical ballet*. New York: Dover Publications.
Graham, M. (1991) *Blood memory; An autobiography*. New York: Doubleday.
— (1965) "How I became a dancer". *Saturday Review*, August 28, p.54.
Grene, M. (1967) Heidegger, Martin. In *The encyclopedia of philosophy* (P. Edwards, Ed.). London: Macmillan.
— (1986) *The mountain of truth: the counterculture begins – Ascona, 1900–1920*. New Hampshire: University Press of New England.
Gropius, W. (1961) (Ed.). *The theater of the Bauhaus*. Middletown, Connecticut: Wesleyan University Press.
Grosz, G. (1983) *An autobiography* (rev. ed., N. Hodges, trans.). New York: Macmillan. (Originally published, 1946).
— (1971) *Ecce Homo*. New York: Dover Publications. (Originally published, 1923).
Gruen, J. (1976) *Interview with Kurt Jooss*. Phonotape, two cassettes, August 3. Dance Collection of The New York Public Library at Lincoln Center.
— (1976) *The private world of ballet*. New York: Penguin Books.
Häger, B. Biography of Kurt Jooss. In *International Encyclopedia of Dance* (S. J. Cohen, Ed.). New York: Macmillan, in press.
Hall, F. (1936) An interview with Jooss. *The Dancing Times*, November.
Haskell, A. (1977) *Balletomania then and now*. New York: Alfred A. Knopf.
Heidegger, M. (1967) *German Existentialism* (D.D. Runes, Ed. and trans.). New York: Philosophical Library.
Helpern, A. (1991) The technique of Martha Graham. *Studies in Dance History*. Pennington: Princeton Periodicals.
Horst, L. (1969) *Modern dance forms in relation to the other modern arts*. New York: Dance Horizons. (Originally published, 1937).

Hodgson, J. and Preston-Dunlop, V. (1990) *Rudolf Laban: introduction to his work & influence.* Plymouth: Northcote House.

Howe, D.S. (1985) *Manifestations of the German Expressionist aesthetic as presented in drama and art in the dance and writings of Mary Wigman.* Unpublished doctoral dissertation, University of Wisconsin-Madison. UMI 8512305.

Hume, M.A.S. (circa 1927) *The court of Philip IV.* London: Eveleigh Nash and Grayson Ltd.

Hutchinson, A. (1955) *The Big City in Labanotation.* Microfilm. The New York Public Library.

— (1955) *The Green Table in Labanotation.* Notated in 1939. Microfilm. The New York Public Library.

— (1977) *Labanotation.* New York: Theatre Arts Books.

— (1954) *Pavane in Labanotation.* Notated in 1938. Microfilm. The New York Public Library.

Huxley, M. (1982) The Green Table, a dance of death: Kurt Jooss in an interview with Michael Huxley. *Balett International*, August-September, pp.8–12.

Hynninem, A. (1974) *Labanotation score of Big City.* Notated in 1974. New York: Dance Notation Bureau.

Isherwood, C. (1952) *Mr. Norris changes trains.* London: The Hogarth Press. (Originally published, 1935).

Jackson, G. (1985) The aesthetic and political origins of European modern dance. *Dance Magazine*, October, pp.44–51.

Jooss, K. (1928) *Choreographische Harmonielehre.* Neue Music-Zeitung (Stuttgart), 49(7).

— (1933) The dance of the future (an interview with Derra de Moroda). *The Dancing Times*, August, pp.453–455.

— (1939) Rudolf von Laban on his 60th birthday. *The Dancing Times*, December, pp.129–131.

Jowitt, D. (1977) *Dance beat: selected views and reviews 1967–1976.* New York: Marcel Dekker.

— (1985) *The dance in mind.* Boston: David R. Gordine.

— (1976) Pavane. *The Village Voice*, March 29, p.94.

Kendall, E. (1979) *Where she danced.* New York: Alfred A. Knopf.

Kessler, H. (1971) *In the twenties* (C. Kessler, trans.). New York: Holt, Reinhart and Winston.

Kirstein, L. (1977) *Dance: a short history of theatrical dancing.* New York: Dance Horizons (Originally published, 1935).

Kisselgoff, A. (1986) Does dance reflect current concerns? *The New York Times*, January 12, section 2, p.18.

— (1985) Experimental dance is not always aided by trappings. *The New York Times*, December 22, section 2, p.7.

— (1982) How much does dance owe to Jooss? *The New York Times*, July 11, section 2, p.17.

— (1988) Pina Bausch adds humor to her palette. *The New York Times*, July 17, section 2, p.9.

— (1989) That German accent in American modern dance. *The New York Times*, February 5, section 2, p.24.

Kleist, H.v. (1955) *Gesammelte Werke.* Berlin: Aufbau-Verlag.

Koch, R. (1988) I'm a playwright of movement. *The New York Times*, March 14, section 2, p.8.

Koegler, H. (1974) In the shadow of the swastika; dance in Germany, 1927–1936. *Dance Perspectives 57.*

Koestler, A. (1969) *Arrow in the blue.* London: Macmillan.

Krasovskaya, V. (1979) *Nijinsky* (J.E. Bowlt, trans.). New York: Macmillan (Originally published, 1974).

Laban, R. (1975) *A life for dance* (L. Ullmann, trans.). London: Macdonald & Evans (Originally published, 1935).

— (1974) *Choreutics* (L. Ullmann, Ed. and trans.). Boston: Plays Inc. (Originally published, 1966).

— (1974) *The language of movement: a guidebook to choreutics* (L. Ullmann, Ed. and trans.). Boston: Plays Inc. (Originally published, 1966).

— (1975) *The mastery of movement* (L. Ullmann, Ed. and trans.). Boston: Plays Inc. (Originally published, 1950).

Lange, R. (1975) (Ed.). *Laban's principles of dance and movement notation* (2nd ed.). Boston: Plays Inc. (Originally published, 1956).

Laqueur, W. (1980) *Weimar: a cultural history, 1918–1933*. New York: Perigee Books (Originally published, 1974).

Langer, R. (1984) The post-war German Expressionism of Pina Bausch and her Wuppertal Dance Theater (R. Sikes, trans.). *Dance Magazine*, June, pp.46–53.

Leatherman, L. (1966) *Martha Graham: portrait of a lady as an artist*. New York: Alfred A. Knopf.

Leeder, S. (1958) Rudolf Laban, an appreciation. *The Dancing Times*, August, p.511.

Levinson, A. (1929) The modern dance in Germany. *Theater Arts*, February, pp.143–153.

Lieven, P. (1973) *The birth of the Ballets-Russes*. New York: Dover Publications.

Litvinoff, V. (1972) *The use of Stanislavsky within modern dance*. New York: American Dance Guild.

Lloyd, M. (1974) *The Borzoi Book of modern dance*. New York: Dance Horizons (Originally published, 1949).

LoMonoco, M.S. (1984) The giant jigsaw puzzle: Robert Joffrey reconstructs Parade. *The Drama Review*, 28(3).

Maas, J. (1983) *Kleist; a biography* (R. Mannheim, trans.). New York: Farrar, Straus and Giroux.

McDonagh, D. (1976) *The complete guide to modern dance*. New York: Doubleday.

— (1970) *The rise and fall and rise of modern dance*. New York: New American Library.

Maletic, V. (1987) *Body space expression: the development of Rudolf Laban's movement and dance concepts*. New York: Mouton de Gruyer.

— (1987) Male-female interaction in dance: probing a methodology for analyzing choreographic intent. In *A spectrum of world dance, Dance Research Annual* (Vol. XVI). New York: CORD.

— (1986) Wigman and Laban: the interplay of theory and practice. *Ballet Review*, 14(3), 86–95.

Manning, S.A. (1986) An American perspective on Tanztheater. *The Drama Review*, 110, pp.67–79.

— (1987) *Body politic: the dances of Mary Wigman*. Unpublished doctoral dissertation, Columbia University, 1987. UMI 8809388.

— (1985) The feminine mystique. *Ballet News*, October, pp.10–17.

Margolis, J. (1965) *The language of art and art criticism*. Detroit: Wayne State University Press.

Marinari, S. (1985) *The Green Table by Kurt Jooss: an example of the new artistic ideas developed in Germany in the first thirty years of the 20th Century*. Unpublished masters thesis, New York University.

Markard, A. (1982) Kurt Jooss and his work. *Ballet Review*, pp.15–67.

— and Markard, H. (1985) *Jooss: Dokumentation von Anna und Hermann Markard*. Köln: Ballett-Bühnen-Verlag.

Marriett, J. (1976) *Labanotation score of A Ball in Old Vienna*. Notated in 1976. New York: Dance Notation Bureau.

Martin, J. (1933) Art of Jooss. *The New York Times*, November 5.

— (1975) *Introduction to the dance*. New York: Dance Horizons (Originally published, 1939).

— (1965) *The modern dance*. New York: Dance Horizons (Originally published, 1933).

Maynard, O. (1965) *American modern dancers: the pioneers*. Boston: Little Brown and Co.

McDonagh, D. (1976) *The complete guide to modern dance*. New York: Doubleday.

— (1973) *Martha Graham: a biography*. New York: Praeger.

Miesel, V. (1970) *Voices of German Expressionism*. Engelwood Cliffs, New Jersey: Prentice-Hall.

Moore, L. (1938) *Artists of the dance*. New York: Dance Horizons.

Morgan, B. (1980) *Martha Graham: sixteen dances in photographs* (rev. ed.). Dobbs Ferry, New York: Morgan and Morgan. (Originally published, 1941).

Moynihan, D.S. and Odom, L.G. (1984) Oskar Schlemmer's Bauhaus dances: Debra McCall's reconstructions. *The Drama Review*, 28(3).

Money, K. (1982) *Anna Pavlova: her life and art*. New York: Alfred A. Knopf.

Moore, L. (1938) *Artists of the dance*. New York: Dance Horizons.

Myers, B.S. (1956) *The German Expressionists: a generation in revolt*. New York: Praeger.

Nadel, M. and Miller, C. (1978) (Eds.). *The Dance Experience*. New York: Universe Books.

Nathanson, L.B. *Interview with Armgard von Bardeleben*. Phonotape. Dance Collection of the New York Public Library at Lincoln Center.

Noverre, J.G. (1968) *Letters on dancing and ballets* (C.W. Beaumont, trans.). New York: Dance Horizons. (Originally published, 1930).

Odom, S.L. (1986) Wigman at Hellerau. *Ballet Review*, 14, 41–53.

Otte-Betz, I. (1938) The work of Rudolf von Laban. *Dance Observer*, December, p.147.

— (1939) The work of Rudolf von Laban II. *Dance Observer*, January, pp.161–162.

— (1939) The work of Rudolf von Laban III. *Dance Observer*, March, pp.189–190.

Percival, J. (1963) Antony Tudor, part one: the use of England. *Dance Perspectives 17*.

— (1971) *The world of Diaghilev*. New York: E.P. Dutton and Co.

Perlmutter, D. (1991) *Shadowplay; The life of Anthony Tudor*. New York: Viking Penguin.

Prevost, N. (1985) Zurich, Dada and dance: formative ferment. *Dance Research Journal*, 17, 3–8.

Raabe, P. (1974) (Ed.). *The era of German Expressionism* (J.M. Ritchie, trans.). New York: The Overlook Press. (Originally published, 1965).

Remarque, E.M. (1958) *All quiet on the western front* (A.W. Wheen, trans.). New York: Fawcett Crest. (Originally published, 1928).

Ritchie, J.M. (1976) *German Expressionist drama*. Boston: Twayne Publishers.

Robertson, A. (1984) Close encounters: Pina Bausch's radical Tanztheater is a world where art and life are inextricably interwoven. *Ballet News*, June, pp.10–14.

Rosenberg, H. (1964) *The anxious object: art and its audience*. New York: Horizon Press.

Rowe, P.A. (1967) *The choreographer's bourne: a theory of aesthetic discipline*. Unpublished doctoral dissertation, Stanford University.

Sachs, C. (1963) *World history of the dance*. New York: W.W. Norton.

Samuel, R. and Thomas, R.H. (1971) *Expressionism in German life, literature and the theatre*. Philadelphia: Albert Saifer.

Scheyer, E. (1970) The shapes of space: the art of Mary Wigman and Oskar Schlemmer. *Dance Perspectives 41*.

Schlemmer, T. (1972) (Ed.). *The letters and diaries of Oskar Schlemmer* (K. Winston, trans). Middletown, Connecticut: Wesleyan University Press.

Schlicher, S. (1987) *Tanztheater Traditionen und Freiheiten Pina Bausch, Gerhard Bohner, Reinhild Hoffmann, Hans Kresnik, Susanne Linke*. Rohwolt Taschenbuch Verlag GmbH: Reinbek bei Hamburg.

Schneede, U.M. (1985) *George Grosz: the artist in his society* (R. Kimber, trans.). New York: Barron's.

Schumacher, G. (1981) *Labanotation score of Pavane on the Death of an Infanta.* Notated in 1981. New York: Dance Notation Bureau.
— (1980–1982) *Labanotation score of The Green Table.* Notated in 1980–1982. New York: Dance Notation Bureau.
Seroff, V. (1971) *The real Isadora: the life of Isadora Duncan.* New York: Avon Books.
Servos, N. (1982) Dance and Emancipation: the Wuppertal Dance Theater. *Ballett International*, January, pp.50–61.
Shawn, T. (1963) *Every little movement: a book about Francois Delsarte.* New York: Dance Horizons. (Originally published, 1910).
— (1979) *One thousand and one night stands.* New York: Da Capo Press. (Originally published, 1960).
Sheets, M. (1978) Phenomenology: an approach to dance. In *The Dance Experience* (M.H. Nadel & C.N. Miller, Eds.). New York: Universe Books.
Shelton, S. (1981) *Divine dancer: a biography of Ruth St. Denis.* New York: Doubleday.
Shirer, W.L. (1960) *The rise and fall of the Third Reich.* New York: Simon and Schuster.
Siegel, M. (1972) *At the vanishing point: a critic looks at dance.* New York: Saturday Review Books.
— (1982) For a minute the smoke clears. *Ballet Review*, pp.33–34.
— (1989) *The Green Table* – sources of a classic. *Dance Research Journal.* Congress on Research on Dance. New York: Spring.
— (1977) *Watching the dance go by.* Boston: Houghton Mifflin.
Soares, J.M. (1992) *Louis Horst: musician in a dancer's world.* Durham: Duke University Press.
Sorell, W. (1981) (Ed.). *Dance in its time.* Garden City: Doubleday.
— (1992) *The dance has many faces* (3rd ed.). New York: Columbia University Press.
— (1971) *The dancer's image: points and counterpoints.* New York: Columbia University Press.
— (1971) (Ed. and trans.). *The Mary Wigman book.* Middletown, Connecticut: Wesleyan University Press.
Sokel, W.H. (1959) *The writer in extremis: Expressionism in twentieth-century German literature.* Stanford: Stanford University Press.
Stanislavsky, C. (1966) *An actor prepares.* New York: Theater Art Books. (Originally Published, 1936).
— (1938) *My life in art* (J.J. Robins, trans.). Boston: Houghton Mifflin.
Stebbins, G. (1977) *Delsarte system of expression.* New York: Dance Horizons. (Originally published, 1902).
— (1974) (Ed.). *"Your Isadora": the love story of Isadora Duncan and Gordon Craig.* New York: Random House.
Steiner, G. (1979) *Martin Heidegger.* New York: The Viking Press.
Stodelle, E. (1978) *The dance technique of Doris Humphrey and its creative potential.* Princeton, New Jersey: Princeton Book Company.
— (1984) *Deep song: the dance story of Martha Graham.* New York: Schirmer Books.
— (1964) *The first frontier: the story of Louis Horst and the American dance.* New York: Morgan Press.
Storey, A. (1940) The art of Kurt Jooss. *The Dancing Times*, July, pp.546–597.
— (1943) Kurt Jooss on mime: the meaning of steps. *The Dancing Times*, July, pp.455–456.
Stuart, V. and Armitage, M. (1970) (Eds.). *The modern dance.* New York: Dance Horizons. (Originally published, 1935).
Taylor, P. (1987) *Private Domain.* New York: Alfred A. Knopf.
Terry, W. (1977) *Ballet guide.* New York: Popular Library.
— (1971) *The dance in America* (rev. ed.). New York: Harper and Row.

— (1967) *Interview with Kurt Jooss*. Phonotape. Dance Collection of the New York Public Library at Lincoln Center.

— (1941) The Jooss Ballet. *New York Herald Tribune*, September 28.

Thornton, S. (1971) *Laban's theory of movement, a new perspective*. Boston: Plays Inc.

Tobias, T. (1988) Bad dreams: Pina Bausch and her Tanztheater Wuppertal. *New York Magazine*, July 25, p.54.

— (1976) *Interview with Kurt Jooss*. Transcript of tape recording, September 26. Oral history project of the Dance Collection of The New York Public Library at Lincoln Center.

Tonnelat, E. (1978) Teutonic Mythology. In *New Larousse Encyclopedia of Mythology*. New York: Hamlyn.

Topaz, M. and Wild, C. (1977) *Labanotation score of The Green Table*. Notated in 1977. New York: Dance Notation Bureau.

Topaz, M. (1989) (Ed.). Antony Tudor: The American Years. *Choreography and Dance*. London: Harwood Academic Publishers.

Tucholsky, K. (1967) *What if? Satirical writings of Kurt Tucholsky* (H. Zohn & K.F. Ross, Eds. and trans.). New York: Funk and Wagnall.

Van Vechten, C. (1974) The dance writings of Carl Van Vechten (P. Padgett, Ed.). New York: Dance Horizons.

Vuillermoz, E. (1932) The Green Table (a review), *Excelsior*, July 24.

Volkonsky, S.M. (1938) Ballets Jooss. *The Dancing Times*, April, pp.25–26.

Wigman, M. (1966) *The Language of dance* (W. Sorell, trans.). Middletown, Connecticut: Wesleyan University Press.

Willett, J. (1978) *Art and politics in the Weimar period: the new sobriety 1917–1933*. New York: Pantheon Books.

— (1970) *Expressionism*. New York: McGraw-Hill.

— (1984) *The Weimar years: a culture cut short*. New York: Abbeville Press.

Winerals, J. (1958) *Modern dance: The Jooss-Leeder method*. London: A.C. Black.

Wingler, H.M. (1984) *The Bauhaus* (W. Jabs & J. Stein, trans.). Cambridge: The MIT Press. (Originally published, 1962).

INDEX

131